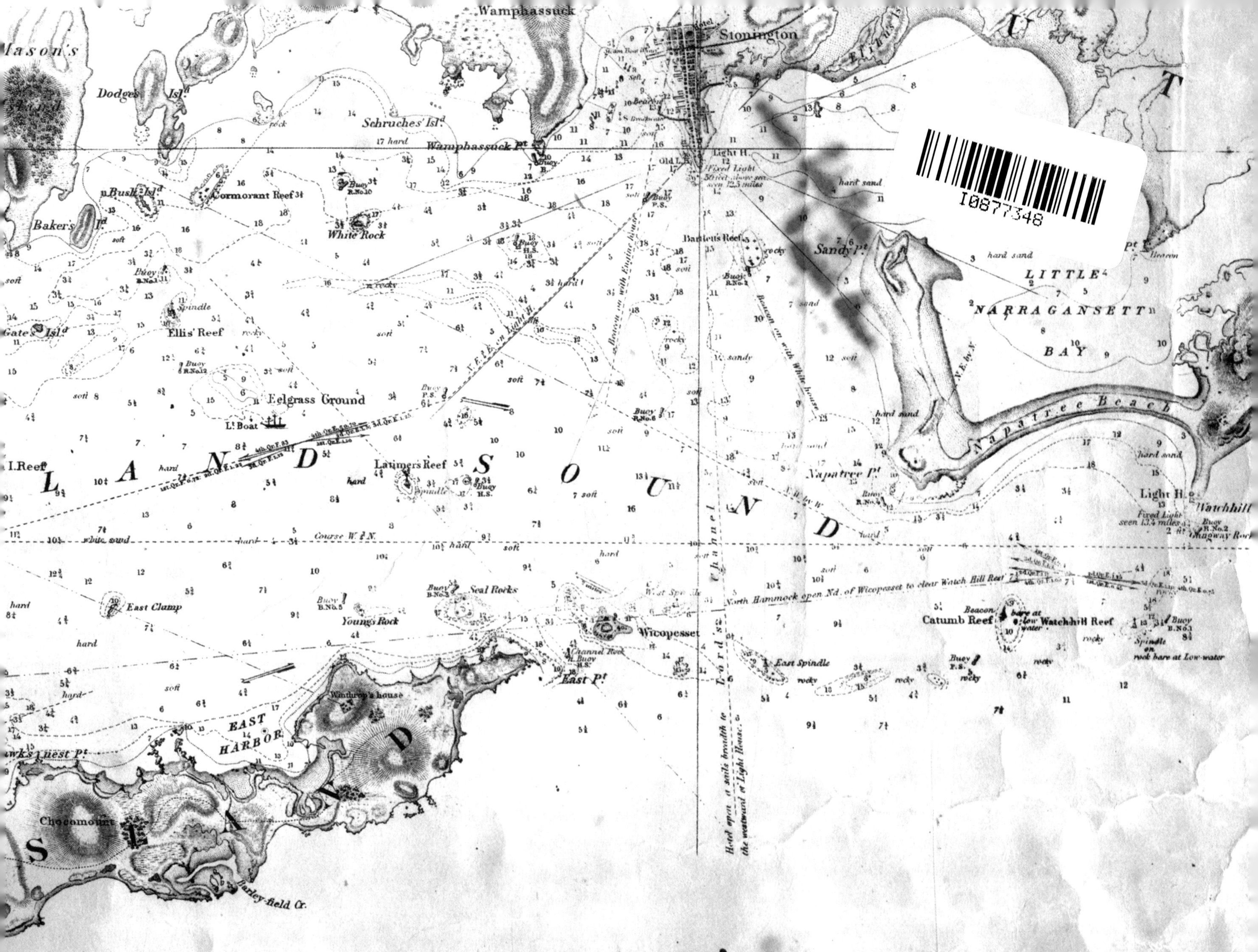

FISHER'S ISLAND SOUND

Founded upon a Trigonometrical Survey

Under the direction of F. R. HASSLER Superintendent of the

SURVEY OF THE COAST OF THE UNITED STATES

Triangulation by W. H. SWIFT Captain Top[l] Engineers

Hydrography by the party under the command of G. S. BLAKE Lieutenant U. S. Navy

Topography by F. H. GERDES Assistant

nel, near East end of Fisher's Island. The mark for this channel is the hotel (a large white build-
at the North end of Stonington) open a sail's breadth to the Westward of Stonington Lt. H.
al other channels through this reef; but having no marks should not be attempted.
ound in from the Ed. when Napatree Pt. bears N.E. by N. steer N.W. by W. for the woods on Mason's
(white stone cone with black barrel on top) is on with a large circular building (engine house) at
steamboat wharf (the Lt. H. bearing N.E. by N. ¼ N.) when run in on that range (course N.E. by E. ½ E.)
round the Breakwater and anchor just far enough in to swing clear of it in 2 fathoms, mud.
ran, when Napatree Point bears N.E. by N. run in with the Easternmost Wh. House on N.W. side of
ith the Beacon on the Breakwater, giving the Lt. H. a berth of ⅛ mile, and leaving Bartlett's Reef
ce to the Eastward.
the Westward. When the Lt. Boat off Bartlett's Reef bears N. ¾ E. distant ¼ mile, steer E. ¾ N. passing
rth Hammock, ¼ mile Sd. of Ram I. Spindle, and about half way between Eel-grass-ground and
, and when Stonington Lt. H. bears N.E. ¾ E. (N. 52° 45' E.) run for it until the Beacon on the
with the large circular building (engine house) at the head of the steamboat wharf, when run
e. At night haul in for the anchorage when ¼ mile from the Lt. H. steering N. by E. ¼ E.
vessels should take pilots before passing the outer Buoy. Vessels drawing not over 10 feet should
ern Buoys 30 yards to the Westward, the Southern Spindle 30 yards to the Ed. and the Spindle
30 yards to the Wd. when haul in N.W. by N. for ¼ mile and follow the West shore along with-
d up with Noank. Above this the channel is too narrow and crooked to be run by directions.
procured at from 1 to 4 dollars.
vard, drawing not over 8 feet, bring Latimer's Spindle half way between Wicopesset and Fisher's I.
ef ¼ mile to the Wd. double round the East Buoy within 30 Yds. steer for the Buoy off the North
hich leave 40 yards to the Sd. & run for the Spindle abreast the Lt. H. keeping it on about half
Lt. H. and the end of the point. As pilotage is here so moderate it is advisable always to take

as three entrances. The Eastern entrance is between Middle Clump and Hawk's Nest Point. Bring
North Hill, run in on that range, doubling round Clay Pt. within 150 Yds. stand in for Mt. Prospect
from 1½ to ¼ fathoms water muddy bottom.

Sailing at Fishers

Sailing at Fishers

A History of the Fishers Island Yacht Club

BY JOHN ROUSMANIERE

Fishers Island Yacht Club, Inc.
Fishers Island, New York
and
Mystic Seaport®
Mystic, Connecticut
2004

Mystic Seaport
75 Greenmanville Ave., P.O. Box 6000
Mystic, CT 06355-0990

Printed in Hong Kong

ISBN 0-939510-93-6 (cloth)
ISBN 0-939511-06-1 (special)

Designed by Darcy Magratten
Printed through InterPress Limited

(Opposite) Saraband.

Courtesy Margaret Scott Ott

Sailing at Fishers

A History of the Fishers Island Yacht Club

CONTENTS

CONTENTS

Sailing at Fishers

A History of the Fishers Island Yacht Club

LANDING IN THE SURF

"An Entirely Different Climate"
The Trials of Sailing at Fishers, 1614-1900

Long before Fishers Island acquired its first yacht club in 1886, boats were sailing on its waters. The earliest one whose name we know was the sloop *Onrust*, in which the Dutch explorer Adrian Block discovered the island in 1614 and named it for his mate, Visschers or the many Indian fishermen he found there. While Block did not leave a record of the sailing conditions, centuries of experience have taught that at Fishers they can range anywhere on the scale from frustrating to challenging to brutally character-building. To quote a present-day Fishers sailor, John Burnham, the only thing predictable about Fishers Island Sound and the Race is "six hours of ebb tide, followed by six hours of flood."

The Quaker missionary George Fox found all this out in 1671 when his ship anchored off "Fisher's" (as it was called before the early twentieth century). The crew and passengers went ashore to sleep, only to be driven back aboard by waves of mosquitoes. Then came the gale. "Next day we went into the Sound," Fox reported, "but finding our sloop was not able to live in that water, we returned again, and came to anchor before Fishers Island, where we lay in our sloop that night also. There fell abundance of rain, and our sloop being open, we were exceedingly wet." No wonder, then, that George Fox was happy to put Fishers in his wake.

With its strong currents, frequent storms, and fringe of rocks and shoals, Fishers Island was never easy to approach by water, especially by the lifeboats cast adrift on its shores following one or another of the many shipwrecks in the Island's history.

G.W. Blunt White Library, Mystic Seaport

The Island's first proprietors, the Winthrops, wrestled with the vagaries of Fishers Island Sound's tides and wind for more than 200 years as they shipped hay and other products from their farms to the mainland. Simply getting themselves out to the Island was often a challenge, too. When John W. Winthrop Jr., tried to introduce his family to Fishers in 1646, they were battered by a storm at sea. A century later, in 1739, some later Winthrops put up with a disorderly cruise to the Island that involved a number of what are now called "weather events." As the family's local agent, Joshua Hempstead, described it in his diary, the cruise started out happily enough as a friendly northerly breeze blew them down the Thames River. Soon, however, they found themselves pounding into a head wind that Hempstead described with some understatement: "Wind came up at SE before night & hindered our Quick passage." Upon reaching the family's homestead near East Harbor, the party was enveloped by "a great & fierce storm from NE to SE."

Here is Hay Harbor in the late nineteenth century, just before Fishers became a resort and sailing center. Used for centuries to harvest hay and pasture horses, sheep, and other livestock, much of the Island was wild, open land. Henry L. Ferguson Museum

There was only one thing to do: "Wee kept house all Day." After the nor'easter blew itself out, the boat was heading back to New London on a favorable flood tide when the weather gods once again refused to cooperate. The tide turned foul, the breeze died, and the boat straggled into Mystic, where the Winthrops finally threw up their hands and rented horses. They eventually reached home 11 hours after weighing anchor at Fishers

Occasionally there were tragedies. In 1723 The Rev. James Pierpont jumped overboard from a disabled Connecticut River ferry and tried to swim ashore. When the impatient cleric washed up at Fishers a month later, he was buried at what came to be called Lone Grave. There he rested for more than two centuries until the 1938 hurricane almost washed him away. He now sleeps high and dry near St. John's Church.

Even the sealife was unpredictable. When a 40-foot sperm whale surfaced in Fishers Island Sound in 1894, fishermen harpooned it and arranged for some oxen to haul the carcass onto a beach in the Island. The whale was eventually towed over to Stonington where for the first time in a generation try-pots were put to work to boil down blubber.

"Until the 1950s," says Charlie Ferguson, "Fishers had the look of Ireland." For almost 150 years the shores of East Harbor, like the rest of the island, still showed the denuding effects of the 1815 hurricane, with only stubby growth. Mystic Seaport 1989.73.7.55

Early Storms

It can be a stormy place. As we will see, the great 1938 hurricane came close to wiping out sailing at Fishers, yet it was hardly the only big blow to affect the Island. A U.S. Navy meteorological study describes the lower Thames River as a "hurricane haven" that between 1886 and 1996 drew a total of 84 tropical storms, including 32 hurricanes. Long before that period, Fishers Island suffered from one of the worst storms in its history. The Great September Gale of September 22-23, 1815, blew for 48 hours, ending with a day-long, vicious southeast blow that kicked up a 17-foot storm surge and blew salt spray so far inland and so heavily that thousands of trees died and wells became brackish. "The heart sickens at the sight," a man from Lyme reported, "...whole forests of trees are either broken down, or torn up by the roots and crossing each other." The storm stripped the Island's slopes naked.

The hills remained that way for more than a century. In a panoramic photograph taken from Reservoir Hill in about 1910, fewer mature trees are visible than sailboats moored in Hay and West harbors. Charles B. Ferguson, who was born on the Island in 1918 and has the eye of both a long-time resident and a painter, wrote in 2000: "Sixty years ago the only 'real' woods were three small

The most notorious wreck in Fishers Island history was the loss, with 45 lives, of the elegant new side-wheeler Atlantic *in 1846 in a Thanksgiving gale. Her anchor now is displayed in front of the Island's school, while her famous tolling bell is in New York.* Mystic Seaport 1945.763

groves at the mid and east end of the Island. The former openness and long inland vistas were more paintable for me than they are now. Until the 1950s, Fishers had the look of Ireland: stone walls, few trees, and windswept moors." Since then, cultivation of new plantings, many of them from seeds blown in by the 1938 hurricane, have returned Fishers to its pre-1815 foliage.

Shipwrecks at Fishers

Sailors at Fishers have had to deal with calms, storms, head winds, head tides, and bugs. And there are the shoals. The 1809 edition of *The American Coast Pilot* urged captains approaching New London to give the Island's western point a vast berth of 3½ miles. "There are several rocks to the westward of it," observed the *Pilot* with a degree of understatement, adding that the channel off that point, called Horse Race, "breaks when there is any wind, especially when it blows against the tide." As for Fishers Island Sound, for years the pilot books damned it with silence, which meant "stay away." Fishers Island was so identified with catastrophe in

THE "*C. VANDERBILT*" ASHORE ON FISHERS ISLAND

The Sound steamer C. Vanderbilt *drifted ashore on Fishers Island in January 1859.* Harper's Weekly *depicted the scene as the vessel lay within sight of her destination on the Connecticut shore and her passengers trudged through the snow to find a vessel to carry them across Fishers Island Sound.*

G.W. Blunt White Library, Mystic Seaport

1852 that a manufacturer of lifeboats recruited testimonials from the men at the Island's three-year-old government lifeboat station, one of the country's first.

The first recorded shipwreck at Fishers was the *John and Lucy*, lost with all her crew in 1671. Eight years later the bark *Providence*, as her captain put it, "fell among a parcell of rocks near Fishers Island Poynt"–that "parcell" may have been Wicopesset Island or Seal Rocks. On Thanksgiving Day, 1846, the disabled 320-foot steamer *Atlantic* dragged anchor and fetched up at North Hill. Forty-five of her 50 people drowned as the ship's bell tolled mournfully. Although it was long thought to have remained at Fishers on "Bell Hill," the *Atlantic*'s bell was acquired not long after the accident by the founder of Seamen's Church Institute of New York, where it hangs to this day. Many years later an anchor believed to be from the *Atlantic* was discovered by Kevin Farrar, a member of the yacht club, while he was scuba diving; he donated this memento of the Island's most famous wreck to the Fishers Island School.

On January 3, 1859, the steamer *C. Vanderbilt* (named for the shipping and railroad tycoon Cornelius Vanderbilt) was making a run from New York to Stonington, where New England trains then terminated, when a thick blizzard closed in and triggered a

As dangerous as Fishers Island Sound is, it was many years before lighthouses were built there. North Dumpling was first lit in 1849 and, with occasional rebuilding and refitting, continues to provide nighttime guidance to mariners. Henry L. Ferguson Museum

series of near-catastrophes that luckily killed nobody. Uncertain of his position, the captain anchored, but the rode snapped and the *Vanderbilt* drifted onto the Island between Race Point and Silver Eel Pond. All 71 passengers and the crew were safely taken off the stranded vessel and, as the captain trudged through the snow in search of rescue, huddled in the lifeboat station for the night, singing psalms before a fire that briefly ignited the roof. Ox-drawn wagons eventually arrived to carry them to West Harbor (which a survivor called "the Mecca of all our hopes") only to discover that the rescue ship had run aground. The frustrated captain eventually found some fishing boats to ferry everyone to Stonington.

"Some Small Bunches of Rocks"

In 1800 a man in the business of laying out privately owned navigation buoys had this to say about Fishers Island Sound: "There are some small bunches of rocks in the Sound, which are always covered at high water, and are much in the way of people coming into the Sound, who are not well acquainted."

Such a warning of the Sound's timeless dangers might still be issued today, when there are many government marks, but two centuries ago, in a time of official indifference to mariners, Fishers Island Sound was a minefield. Only a few rocks were marked with lengths of iron (called spindles if they carried identifying marks or spears if they were naked), but even if they were not bent or swept away by storms or ice, both were useless in poor visibility because they were unlit. A point of land might be marked by a beacon, which was nothing more than a pile of rocks on which fires were lit. The first lighthouses at the western and eastern entrances to the Sound were New London (first lit in 1760) and Watch Hill (1807). Stonington Point got a light in 1823, but most of the channels and harbors within the Sound remained unmarked for decades, even though thousands of ships and boats were passing by the reefs every year from the early nineteenth century on

Local sailors knew the Sound and its tides intimately. A trick of Noank fishermen heading out to sea was to sail over to Fishers' East Point in the evening, anchor overnight in Money Pond Bay (where Captain William Kidd was believed to have buried treasure), and catch the first of the morning ebb tide to hasten their passage. Visiting captains, however, required guidance, which the government was slow to provide even as the Sound became crowded with commercial vessels. It took a privately owned shipping company to set out the first light within Fishers Island

At a time when thousands of commercial and pleasure vessels sailed up and down the Sound every year, the tricky north side of the Sound was marked by large, sturdy lightships, including ones at Eel Grass Shoal and (shown here) Ram Island Reef.

Henry L. Ferguson Museum

Sound. This was a small boat that was anchored north of Flat Hammock in 1837 to guide steamboats to and from the railhead at Stonington. The government Light House Service finally replaced it 12 years later when it bought North Dumpling Island from the Winthrops and built a lighthouse there

Neglect of the Sound's shoals continued. When a journalist standing on a Fishers Island hill in 1881 spotted 19 lighthouses, only one (North Dumpling) was in Fishers Island Sound. Latimer Reef, at the eastern end of the main channel, did not get a light until 1884. The channel's northern boundary was finally lit two years later when a lightship was anchored off Ram Island.

Entering Fishers Island's burgeoning commercial port was an adventure as late as the 1880s. This was West Harbor, which was then often called Great Hay Harbor to reflect one of the Island's main exports in the Winthrop years. In the 1880s the harbor was a busy place. Steam ferries called several times a day, fishing boats came out of Pirate's Cove, barges serviced the Sage Brick Works on the harbor's southeast shore, and there was a small anchorage for the big steam yachts that could not fit into shallow Little Hay Harbor. Yet as busy as it was, West Harbor—from its inner shore out to and across its wide, treacherous rock-strewn mouth—was marked by only one government buoy, located off North Hill. Today, the area has eleven buoys, six of them in the harbor mouth alone. Following years of appeals by businessmen, the Island's proprietors, and elected officials, the Light House Service in 1889 finally agreed to put out more buoys. With these new aids to navigation, West Harbor became more accessible not only to commercial vessels, but also to yachts.

By far the most astounding feat of marking channels in the area was the creation in the 1870s of Race Rock Light. Captain Thomas A. Scott built it on a wave-swept ledge just off the western tip of Fishers Island.

Henry L. Ferguson Museum

Only a spindle marked Race Rock in the area's most dangerous body of water, Horse Race (now called the Race), off the Island's western end. In 1871 the government decided to try to build a lighthouse on Race Rock. The job was handed to a salvager from New Jersey who had a reputation for bravado of a reckless if not suicidal kind (he had plugged a big leak in a Hudson River ferry by squeezing his body into the hole). "No man or child could look Captain Thomas A. Scott in the face without instantly believing in him," observed the Race Rock light supervisor, F. Hopkinson Smith, "and no act of his in after life would shake that belief." Working year-round for seven years, Scott constructed a concrete foundation below the water surface and then put the lighthouse on it. After the light went into service in 1878, Scott set up shop in New London as an underwater contractor and salvager. Many of the 500 wrecks that his company salvaged were on the shores and shoals of Fishers Island.

While mariners welcomed these aids to navigation, some annoyed landspeople. After Ledge Light was given a loud siren, a New London politician complained that its "horrible shrieking and groaning" would scare away tourists. "Our summer colony has begun to arrive for rest and recuperation and unless something is done pretty soon, this will be the best field of practice for a specialist of nervous disease that I know of." Against the protests of Captain Scott and other mariners, the Light House Service, for once acting promptly, replaced the siren with a less abrasive horn.

While the Island's first proprietors, the Winthrops, had small passenger vessels, the first yacht known to be regularly moored at Fishers was Faye Fox, *owned by Robert R. Fox. After his death in 1871, his family began to convert the Island from farming to the tourist trade—the step that led in time to founding a yacht club.*

Henry L. Ferguson Museum

The First Yachts

Until Fishers began to be developed as a resort in the late 1870s, it had no services ashore to handle the needs of visiting sailors. The Island's chief role in early yachting history was to serve as a turning mark for racing boats. That was not always easy. One year, the Sound was so messy with what a newspaperman described as "baffling winds, calms, and fogs" and "simply villainous" conditions that many entries in the New York Yacht Club's annual cruise anchored rather than risk being swept upon the clumps and hammocks.

The first yacht moored at Fishers seems to have been owned by the man who bought the Island from the Winthrops in 1863. Intending to build a large manor farm, Robert R. Fox, a retired New York merchant, accumulated a fleet to carry animals and people to and from the mainland. *Faye Fox*, a sloop-rigged yacht of unknown dimensions and named for the owner's daughter, was used by the family. After Fox's death in 1871, his heirs gave up on his farm scheme and, with the help of the family trustee, James Lyles, came up with a plan for development, a big part of which was tourism. Promising in promotional brochures that "The tranquil waters of Fisher's Island Sound gently ebb and flow upon the beach," they built cottages near Little Hay Harbor, a resort hotel, Lyles Beach, near North Hill, and, for the staff, the three identical cottages now called the Three Sisters. Excursion steamers brought daytrippers across from the mainland to what the hotel's manager, Paul Green, called "this Beautiful Isle of the Sea." Lyles Beach had a capacious restaurant, a dance hall, a bowling alley, a skating rink, a billiard room, a shooting gallery, and a two-ring circus called the "Paris Hippodrome" featuring bareback riders, a Japanese juggler, and, on occasion, a two-headed woman named Millie Christine.

For many day-trippers, the main appeal was Lyles Beach's saloon. Eastern Connecticut lay under the rigid influence of a fervid prohibitionist named Hugh Montgomery, and thirsty Nutmeggers developed a keen affection for this nearby piece of New York. A newspaper jokingly proposed that Connecticut annex Fishers Island so it could "extend the benefits of Brother Montgomery's moral supervision; at present they get on very well without it." Paul Green cagily played both sides of the street by advertising the availability of his resort for Sunday school picnics.

LADIES TO RACE YACHTS.

NEW-LONDON, Conn., July 21.—Everybody is interested here just now in tub and boat racing. On Wednesday next there is to be a 10-mile catboat race, a tub race, and a clam bake at Fisher's Island. A particularly novel feature of the boat race will be the entries of two boats to be sailed by two young ladies, Miss Faye Fox and Miss Kate Hurlburt. It will be a great day for the island. The two lady yachtsmen will undertake a feat never before recorded in these parts. The idea of a woman sailing a craft in a yacht race is taking, and the popular hope is that one or both will be successful. Miss Fox is a handsome young lady, who has always lived on the island except while being educated. She is the heir to that insular Eden and a very skillful boatwoman. Miss Hurlbut is a Summer boarder there and also equally skillful at sea.

The Lyles Beach hotel attracted day-trippers and overnight guests who were drawn to its attractive location, its varied amusements, and its alcoholic beverages. Henry L. Ferguson Museum

Among Green's promotions was boating. Guests of Lyles Beach could go down to the landing and find a boat captained by a fisherman to take them sailing or fishing. There also were races to watch. Some were serious competitions between fishermen in catboats or village champions in rowboats. Others were hilarious contests between ordinary tin washtubs filled with madly paddling men struggling to get around the course before capsizing.

Something different was scheduled for July 23, 1884. Three steamboats carried 900 people from Norwich and New London down to Lyles Beach to enjoy a clambake and watch what Green had promoted as "the grand regatta." On the schedule were the usual tub and rowboat races, and also a special event—a sailboat race between two women skippers, Faye Fox and a summer cottager, Kate Hurlbut. "It will be a great day for the Island," ran a story in the *New York Times*. "The two lady yachtsmen will undertake a feat never before recorded in these parts. The idea of a woman sailing a craft in a yacht race is taking, and the popular hope is that one or both will be successful." The *Times* did not try to explain how both skippers could win, but the good feeling was clear enough. As it turned out, the "grand regatta" did not occur and the women did not sail. But that such a thing was even considered revealed possibilities for the future.

Although women played a prominent role on the water from the early days of sailing at Fishers, it is a safe bet that these elaborately dressed, somewhat anxious-looking ladies were posing for the camera and not about to climb aboard a typical late-nineteenth-century catboat.

Henry L. Ferguson Museum

In this typical waterfront scene, taken on West Harbor around 1900, there is not an engine in sight. Most of these boats probably carried hotel guests on short excursions.

Henry L. Ferguson Museum

The Ubiquitous Catboat

The least surprising thing about the proposed race between Faye Fox and Kate Hurlbut was that it was in catboats. The nineteenth century's equivalent of the Boston Whaler as the utility vessel of choice, the catboat was a fat little vessel between about 14 and 30 feet in length and had a single gaff-headed sail. With its large capacity and simple rig, it was a favorite for one-man fishing. Come summer, a fisherman might clean up his boat until she looked "almost like a yacht," as one of them, Howard Burdick, recalled. He would make an arrangement with Lyles Beach or one of the Island's later hotels—the Mononotto, Munnatawket, and Mansion House—to take charter parties out for sightseeing, fishing in the Race, or (in the case of a few men) a little private partying over a bottle, far from the constraints of wives, children, and prohibitionists.

Awkward as they may appear today, catboats could be extremely agile. "It was amazing to see how they were handled," a long-ago historian wrote of a fleet of cats serving as launches at Newport. "Skipper and crew consisted of one man, yet they worked their way through the maze of yachts and trading vessels anchored in the little harbor, with or without breeze, and without ever scraping the paint off anything. It was wonderful to see those clumsy-looking boats with no other means of propulsion than a single sail, moving with no perceptible air, silently, yet surely, through the narrowest and crookedest lanes between anchored yachts."

Scenes like that would have been common on Fishers Island Sound, where there were many catboats. Here is a newspaper report concerning Noank in 1896:

A fine new catboat for William Hills of Fishers Island was launched Saturday from the W. Charles Smith boatyard. She is 24 feet overall and 11 feet beam. The boat has been built with particular reference to Mr. Hills's taste for fishing and pleasure sailing and she is as handsome a craft as any man could desire. This is the fifth boat of the class that Mr. Smith has turned out this season and he has every right to be proud of the production of his skill. The boat was built entirely by Mr. Smith and Earnest Davis and she is fitted out together in a manner that challenges any one's skill in this part of the country to excel...

Perhaps that handsome catboat spent some of her days in the charter business at Fishers.

A pair of cheerful day-trippers from Connecticut picnic on their cat-rigged boat on a shore of Fishers Island, with one of the Island's few standing trees in the background. The outfits would seem ridiculously formal today but were typical back then. Mystic Seaport 1989.73.7.43

The First Fishers Island Yacht Club

As the Foxes and James Lyles were developing Fishers Island, interest in yachting bubbled up among summer people and a few men who had stakes in the Island's future. On March 22, 1886, a certificate of incorporation for the Fisher's Island Yacht Club was filed in Brooklyn, New York. This club quickly disappeared, however, and in its story we can see again that sailing at Fishers did not come easily.

All but one of this first yacht club's five founders were involved with the Island's development. One was the Fox family's executor, James Lyles. Another, William Hoies, was a lawyer who would soon represent Edmund M. and Walton Ferguson when they purchased Fishers Island from the Foxes. A third, Henry Bowers, was a New London contractor who owned and rented out several of the cottages that the Foxes had built.

The only founders known to be enthusiastic sailors were Edward and George Bartlett, two middle-aged brothers from Pennsylvania who were Henry Bowers's nephews. Edward, who apparently had no financial interest in the Island, practiced law in Brooklyn and often sailed up to Fishers. George seems to have been the key figure in the first yacht club. He was a summer resident, he co-founded St. John's Church (his father, The Rev. Josiah M. Bartlett, was the first rector), and he invested in the Island by buying several Fox cottages. When Edmund M. Ferguson paid what may have been his first visit to Fishers, in 1883, he came up in his big steam yacht and rented one of George Bartlett's cottages.

This first Fishers Island Yacht Club was tied to the commercial enterprise of developing Fishers as a resort. Like an Episcopal chapel, a yacht club would attract middle-class families while signaling that the Island was stable and respectable. Two years later, a Sportsmen's Club was founded to attract people to the Island, usually in the fall or early winter, to fish, conduct field trials, or hunt birds.

The Foxes and their partners faced plenty of competition. Across America, there was an explosion of resorts and yacht and golf clubs on land that had been made accessible by new railroads and ferry lines. The first American yacht clubs were city institutions founded in the 1830s and '40s in Boston, Detroit, New York, and Halifax, Nova Scotia (the oldest U.S. yacht club in continuous existence is the New York Yacht Club, founded in 1844). By 1886 well over 100 yacht clubs were thriving around the United States in suburbs and at summer places from New England to California. A typical story is that of the 11 sailing vacationers at a Methodist seaside resort on the eastern end of Long Island who, needing someone to start and finish their sailboat races, founded the Shelter Island Yacht Club in 1886. It has been thriving ever since.

If the new Fishers Island Yacht Club was less successful, it was because the need was not as specific as at Shelter Island. In fact, the club instantly vanished. Except for a mention in a yachting column in a New York newspaper and a copy of its incorporation papers in the present-day yacht club's archives, no trace of it can be found. The only possible explanation is that it did not fit local needs except the ambitions of its founders. Their goal, as laid out in the certificate of incorporation, was broad and bland: "The encouragement and development of the recreation of yachting at Fisher's Island." Later came a statement hinting at something more concrete, and also more ambitious: "a branch office may be established at the city of New York." Very likely that was to be a second clubhouse or gathering place in the city, where several founders (and many potential summer people) worked or lived. At that time, a few suburban yacht clubs had both waterfront and city clubhouses, but those clubs—including New York, New Bedford, American, and Seawanhaka Corinthian—were headquartered in major yachting centers, which Fishers Island was yet to become. That would happen in the 1920s.

There is good evidence that even its founders decided that the club was premature. In the 1887 edition of *The American Yacht List*, Edward Bartlett's entry for his sloop *Ibis* does not list a yacht club, even though he had co-founded one at Fishers Island just a year earlier. His brother George, meanwhile, kept his boats on the mainland and did not say a word about the club either in his extensive correspondence or in his 1895 novel about Fishers and sailing, *Water Tramps*. The only boat with a Fishers Island hailing port in the 1887 *Yacht List* was a sloop owned by Walton Ferguson, who with his brother was negotiating to acquire the Island.

This lack of interest is understandable given the lack of local demand for races, an anchorage, launch service, instruction, and the other services that a yacht club provides. While some privately owned boats were moored at the Island in the late nineteenth century, most summer residents were cottage renters whose interest in sailing was well satisfied by chartering a fisherman's catboat for an afternoon. Much the same could probably be said about the entire Fishers Island Sound area. While there had been hotels at Ram Island and Watch Hill as early as the 1850s, the region did not become a major center for vacationers and summer cottagers until the end of the century. On the heels of the construction of the casinos came sailing programs and yacht clubs. The earliest permanent yacht club at a local summer place apparently was the Wadawanuck Club, which was founded at Stonington in 1895. At that time the members of the Noank Yacht Club were gathering in a spare room in a ship chandlery to organize catboat races. The Watch Hill Yacht Club did not appear until 1913.

By then Fishers had its first established yacht club, although it was not a yacht club in name. This was the Hay Harbor Club. Founded in 1908 in the former home of James Lyles's daughter, it served as the Island's sailing center for 20 years, when (as we will see) another generation of sailors with ambitions very different from George Bartlett's took the step of founding another, more permanent Fishers Island Yacht Club at West Harbor.

Shallow, well-protected Hay Harbor served the maritime interests not only of the many guests of the large Mononotto Inn (in the background) but of the growing number of summer residents like William Gaillard, who first came to Fishers in 1909. Here he is with his children in a skiff.

Courtesy of M. Lee Gaillard

"An Ideal Summer Resort"

Before yachting could become popular, Fishers had to become a full-fledged summer place. After Robert Fox's widow, Eliza, died in 1886, it took a while to sort out her estate, whose complications she had blamed on her family's legal advisors ("I particularly desire that no lawyers shall have anything to do with this document," she wrote in her will.) Three years later, most of Fishers Island was acquired for $250,000 by Edmund and Walton Ferguson, who had recently sold their coke business to Andrew Carnegie.

The Fergusons, both of whom were yachtsmen, envisioned making Fishers into a classy summer haven for people who, like them, loved the water. "The place seems to be an ideal summer resort," Edmund announced to a newspaper; "in addition to the boating, bathing, fishing, and hunting, cool sea breezes fan the Island, and flies and mosquitoes are unknown." Daytrippers became a memory when the Fergusons replaced the tacky Lyles Beach Hotel with the more upscale Munnatawket, meanwhile gaining control of waterborne access to the Island by acquiring underwater land out to 200 feet from shore. They hired Thomas A. Scott, the builder of Race Rock Light, to tear down the old Lyles Beach wharf so it could be replaced by a grander structure to accommodate large yachts.

Tub races may have disappeared with the two-headed woman, but not sailing. The catboat charter business was allowed to survive. In 1893 the hotel's brochure promised rides in "some of the fastest sailing boats on the Sound" commanded by "old and experienced captains ready to take parties out for a pleasure sail or fishing excursion." A tourist who was not interested in sailing "can sit and watch the white winged yachts go sailing by." Not long after that, the Mononotto Inn was built on a hill above Hay Harbor, where there were beaches, piers, and plenty of boats.

These well-dressed young yachtsmen and many subsequent generations of young summer sailors have learned the art of boathandling at the Hay Harbor Club, which was founded in 1908, served as the Island's yacht club for 20 years, and still is the center for teaching basic sailing. Henry L. Ferguson Museum

The busy Munnatawket Hotel wharf was the ferry landing until the 1938 hurricane, as well as a center for charter boat operation. Henry L. Ferguson Museum

Fishers had "an entirely different climate" George Bartlett observed in his book Water Tramps. *A founder of the first, very short-lived yacht club at Fishers, Bartlett made the island and its harbors the center of his ambitious but low-budget sailing and fishing activities.*

Henry L. Ferguson Museum

The First Yachtsman: George Bartlett

"The steamer *Skipjack* towed the Fishers Island scow down yesterday," the *New London Day* reported early in the summer of 1884. "It was loaded with the horses, carriages, and household goods of Messrs. Bowers and Bartlett, bound for their summer residences on the Island." Two years later Henry Bowers and George H. Bartlett helped found the Island's first yacht club. Bowers was important in the Island's history because of his relationship with the Fergusons, but Fishers Island's first true yachtsman was George Bartlett.

A traveling salesman based in Bethlehem, Pennsylvania, and New York, he first came to the Island accidentally in 1864 when his boat was dismasted and blown out of the Thames River down onto Fishers. He returned in a more permanent fashion later on, but spent much of his summers in his boats. We know he was a fanatical sailor from an exchange between a landsman and Bartlett's hero in his novel, *Water Tramps*:

> "Is there anything that occurs on a sailboat that you don't find enjoyable?"
>
> "I don't think of anything just now, unless it is a dead calm in a hot sun. Even that has its bright side."

To a passionate sailor, that response by Bartlett's surrogate is as satisfying as the sailing writer R.T. McMullen's favorable comparison of going cruising under sail with "successfully gathering roses off thorns."

While Edward Bartlett remained faithful to one boat for years, his younger brother George owned a long string of small cruising sailboats, some of them oddly named. *Umbrella, Albatross, Dream, Penguin, White Wing, Aylwyn*, and the others were all simple and inexpensive. He sold *Umbrella* for all of $55. They were cheap to maintain, too. After *White Wing* suffered some damage below the waterline in 1887, Bartlett paid $5.75 for repairs at a yard in Noank (75 cents was the cost of the labor). He loved to cruise and fish for bluefish and mackerel in the Race. Bartlett liked a good blow and seems to have had a cast-iron stomach to go with it. One windy September afternoon in 1884, he sailed into New London so oblivious to the prevailing conditions that he was surprised to find the storm flag flying. In a letter home, he summarized that day's activities this way: "The *Dream* sailed beautifully. We fixed fried oysters, chops, tea, and coffee on the boat."

Bartlett wrote two novels that tell a little of his and Fishers Island's world at the end of the nineteenth century. His first, titled *A Commercial Trip, with an Uncommercial Ending*, published in 1884, is a comedy of a commercial traveler's life with the romantic additions of plenty of music, a charming young woman (whose agreement to marry the hero provides the "uncommercial ending"), and several pleasurable rides on boats. Some people are addicted to wine, women, and song. Bartlett's joy was the triad of song, women, and the sea.

Bartlett's second book, *Water Tramps, or the Cruise of the Sea Bird*, which he paid to have published in 1895, is the one about sailing near Fishers. The "tramps" (by which he meant "travelers," not "bums") are a law student named Harold Allen, three other men, and a dog named Captain, all packed into a small sloop on an impecunious summer's cruise financed by selling the fish they catch along the way. They negotiate with stubborn watermen, flirt with girls from a luxury steam yacht owned by a family named Turner, take the girls on a sail from New London to Little Hay Harbor, meet some eccentric fishermen-clergymen, make some rescues, and do lots of sailing near Fishers. But nowhere is there a mention of a sailboat race or a yacht club.

Water Tramps appears to be George Bartlett's last published book. He died on the Island in 1918 and is buried in the St. John's cemetery. His daughter Winifred Stockbridge Bartlett Shaw Clark, another writer, lived on the Island for many years and is buried near him.

Sailing to Fishers Island in the 1890s

In this charming excerpt from *Water Tramps*, George Bartlett describes a short co-ed voyage from New London into "an entirely different climate" at Fishers.

It was a sail of about eight miles. Never before had the students taken so much pains to make the little yacht look attractive. They had spent two dollars for cut flowers with which to decorate the cabin. Captain had a new blue ribbon around his neck, which was very becoming to him and set off his beautiful brown color to advantage.

It was a very warm day ashore, the thermometer registering 92 in the shade at New London. The students had put up a small awning, which they had often found gave them real comfort when the wind was light and the sun hot. Going down the harbor they sailed close to two of the new battleships. As they passed out of New London Harbor into the Sound it became cooler, and soon they seemed to have sailed into an entirely different climate. The breeze was still a land breeze in New London, but it was delightfully cool by the time it reached the Sea Bird.

The Turners had made arrangements for boarding at a cottage settlement on Little Hay Harbor. Harold consulted his chart and found that the inlet into this little harbor was narrow and not very deep, and he scarcely knew whether it were wise to attempt entering with the Sea Bird. *The chart showed plainly that large vessels could go into West Harbor, but that would not be as convenient for the Turners.*

"I will keep on until we reach the mouth of Little Hay Harbor," said Harold; "and as the wind is light and fair, I think I can feel my way in and land you close to your cottage."

When the Sea Bird *arrived off Little Hay Harbor, Harold luffed up alongside of a small fishing boat in which there was a man hauling lobster pots.*

"Can we get into Little Hay Harbor?" asked Harold.

"Not unless you know the way in," said the man. "There is only about two feet of water, at this stage of the tide, in the middle of the channel. How much water are you drawing?"

"About three feet," said Harold.

"You will have to hold on a while, then," said the man. "I'm going in pretty soon. The tide is rising. I shall be glad to pilot you in as soon as I've hauled my lobster pots."

With the Little Hay Harbor pilot aboard, they sailed safely in, and the Sea Bird *was tied up to a little wharf within a stone's throw of the cottage which the Turners were to occupy. This cottage was one of a group, convenient to which was a building containing a large dining room, etc., where the cottagers had their meals. The students were charmed by the harbor and its surroundings.*

It was a beautiful spot. The land lay high and rolling, and many cottages dotted the knolls A pretty church stood upon a hill not far off—St. John's Episcopal, as they soon learned.

The Harbor was completely land-locked, except for the narrow inlet, and seemed like a lake. A number of sailboats lay either at their moorings, or were sailing back and forth in the harbor. The banks were green, the birds singing, and the shore was a garden of wild flowers.

"This is different from any place we have struck before," said Harold, "And I wish we could stay for a week at least. But we must not forget that we are not exactly loaded down with wealth. We must stick to the fishing business."

George Bartlett's big catboat Penguin *glides into an uncrowded, undeveloped Hay Harbor in the 1890s. Change was coming.* Henry L. Ferguson Museum

"It Was a Getaway"
Fishers Becomes a Sailing Center, 1900-1938

Edmund Ferguson, with his brother Walton, founded the new Fishers Island summer colony. Henry L. Ferguson Museum

(Left) "Here is perfect quiet," Rufus Bradford Burnham wrote after discovering West Harbor as a cruising port in 1911. Here in his photograph of the family's 28-foot sloop, Querida IV, *his wife, Louise Campbell Burnham, steers alongside their children Brad and Helen. Today, their brother David's Bullseye is named* Querida. Rufus Bradford Burnham photo

After almost three hundred years of isolation, Fishers in the late nineteenth century was becoming both a successful resort and a yachting center. The Ferguson brothers believed that the two went hand in hand. At the time they acquired most of the Island from the Fox estate in 1889, the dispute about improving West Harbor's accessibility was at its peak. Edmund Ferguson made his concern clear in a succinct public statement: "Mr. Ferguson intends to make the Island attractive to yachtsmen."

Such resolve on the part of the Island's new proprietor must not have hindered the improvement of West Harbor as an attractive yacht anchorage. A first step was placing several buoys to set apart the barges that lay off the Sage Brick Works located on the harbor's southeast shore at the site of the present-day Grey Gulls estate. The Works manufactured as many as 15 million bricks a year from clay dug from Island pits. When the Brick Works was shut down around 1908, the anchorage not only gained more room for yachts but became far more quiet and clean. In fact it was so quiet that in 1911 a visiting writer in a boat, Rufus Bradford Burnham, heard Taps played at Fort Wright, two miles away. "Here is perfect quiet," Burnham wrote in a boating magazine, "with no disturbing swell, noise, or inquisitive prowler, and the bugle notes from the fort sound enchanting as they are borne through the calm air." Burnham later bought a house on the Peninsula in West Harbor, where, long after Fort H.G. Wright was decommissioned, his sons Brad and David and their children and grandchildren enjoyed hearing the chimes of Union Chapel as they spent their summers messing about in all sorts of boats.

Walton Ferguson was a leader in the rise of yachting at Fishers.

Henry L. Ferguson Museum

The Fergusons and Their Boats

Under the Fergusons, Fishers Island acquired an identity that was crucial for any upscale resort in the age of Theodore Roosevelt—a setting for vigorous outdoors activity. Consider the following breathless promotion from a 1920s brochure for the Mansion House, the most stylish of the three hotels: "There isn't a dull moment for anyone who cares to walk, drive, or ride; bathe, sail, row, or fish; play golf, tennis, or croquet." Boats got top billing. Seven of the brochure's 16 photographs showed sailboats, and only four showed golfers.

Salt water ran in the Fergusons' blood. In 1866 their uncles Henry and Samuel took to a lifeboat from a burning ship in the Pacific with ten days' provisions. On the 42nd day they saw a double rainbow, which the captain called "the bow of promise," and a day later they came ashore at Hawaii and told their story of sailing 4,000 miles in an open boat to Samuel L. Clemens, who retold it in newspaper articles.

(Left) *Walton Ferguson's stylish 164-foot steam yacht* Christabel *was designed by G.L. Watson and constructed at Glasgow, Scotland, in 1893. She even had electric lights.* James Burton photo. 1984.187.B246, © Mystic Seaport, Rosenfeld Collection

(Above) *In their summer yachting attire, the Ferguson family and their friends enjoy the comforts of* Christabel*'s quarterdeck.* Henry L. Ferguson Museum

Between them the brothers owned a number of boats, including a big schooner named *Vega*, a small sloop, and three large steam yachts that sometimes tied up in Hay Harbor when there was enough water. Walton's steamer *Christabel* was shallow, but not shallow enough. On the evening of June 23, 1909, he was proudly watching her steam into Hay Harbor to pick up his party to watch the Harvard-Yale boat races at New London when she fetched up on a ledge. Even the ferry *Munnatawket* couldn't get her off immediately, and so one of the owners of Fishers Island had to await the next flood tide before he could attend the races.

Fergusons were well represented in the second, permanent Fishers Island Yacht Club, which was founded in 1928. In 1931, 14 senior or junior members—over 12 percent of the total membership—were members of the family. The diverse Ferguson fleet in 1934 included Sally's Skiddoo *Rangerette*, Vaughan's eye-catching Alden schooner *Mary Leigh*, and Alfred's sturdy powerboat *Hawk*. Walton's grandson Charlie Ferguson, already fascinated by boats, built himself an eight-foot dinghy in shop class and sailed it on Middle Farm Pond when he wasn't crewing in Bullseyes and Luders 16s. He launched his long career as a fisherman in his uncle's *Hawk*, when Captain Olaf Jensen taught him to troll with handlines for blues in the Race and catch tuna and swordfish off Montauk. Charlie Ferguson was still on the water seven decades later, and he won the last race of the Bullseye National Championship in 2002.

A Catboat Class for Hay Harbor

In 1910 Fishers Island acquired the first of its many racing sailboat classes, the Fishers Island One Design, in which two generations of sailors got a feel for the Island's tricky waters.

But before the FIOD there was a little catboat in which three generations of Islanders learned to sail. The origins of the Skiddoo, which many Islanders loved to hate, are lost in time. Its name is ironic if not sarcastic. "Skiddoo" was a popular term in the 1920s, "23 skiddoo" meant something like "beat it." The distinctly slow Skiddoo—for some reason pronounced "Skiddooie"—probably began life in one of the small boatyards that lined every New England port. Noank alone had some two dozen such shops in the late nineteenth and early twentieth centuries. It is not inconceivable that one of those two-man operations produced the Skiddoo to satisfy a commission by the Mononotto Inn or another hotel that needed a safe, slow, cheap catboat for its guests to sail on Hay Harbor or some other placid water.

Except for two features, the Skiddoo was similar to many New England catboats, like the Beetle Cat. What distinguished it were, first, the triangular leg o' mutton (Marconi) mainsail instead of a gaff-headed sail, and, second, its lapstrake construction, with the planks overlapping instead of laid edge to edge. This rig and building method were cheap. New Skiddoos probably cost well under $200; perhaps even less if bought in large numbers. The Skiddoo was the launching pad for young sailors for 30 years until they finally wore out in the late 1930s.

"Master Nicholas Has Gone Yachting" and Other Tales of the Skiddoo

"It was a marvelously heavy, heavy boat with a centerboard and one sail—a tub, like a picture in a children's book." (Jean McIntire Leuchtenburg)

"It was a horrible little boat. One day, after a lesson with the Campbell Soup heiress [a Dorrance], the halyard went up the mast while at anchor. Petey Talbot yelled, 'Shinny up the mast, Charlie, and get it.' I did, and the Skiddoo slowly capsized with me at the top of the mast!" (Charlie Ferguson)

"I started in the Skiddoo fleet at Hay Harbor. Mostly what I remember is how easy they were to capsize. Also, we ran aground a lot. I really don't remember any of the sailing instructors, but there was one amusing incident. My family had a Welshman as a butler, Allen by name. Very proper. A friend called up to speak with me. I was out having a sailing lesson. Allen allegedly replied, 'Master Nicholas has gone yachting.'" (Nick Brown)

(Opposite) *As tubby little Skiddoos career about in Hay Harbor, the only people in full control are the girls in the rowboat.*

(This page) *With their lapstrake planking, leg o mutton (Marconi) mainsail, and heavy construction, the Skiddoos were fixtures of the Island's sailing program until the eve of World War II. As the accompanying quotes indicate, they were not widely beloved.* Courtesy M. Lee Gaillard

The Fishers Island One Design

In 1909, some members of the new Hay Harbor Club decided to introduce a modern racing sailboat. One-design classes were a relatively novel thing at that time, but several yacht designers had come up with able boats, some in keel versions for clubs fronting on deep water, others with centerboards for shallow waters like Hay Harbor. The Fishers sailors went to one of the country's best young yacht designers, Charles D. Mower, of whom it was said, "He never designed a slow boat or a homely one." Raised in Massachusetts and working in New York and Philadelphia, Mower specialized in centerboarders. Having experience with the modern extreme racing boats, he proposed a 38-foot scow with a flat bottom and an immense spread of canvas on a gaff-headed rig. With a modern Marconi rig, this boat would be a dead ringer for a modern-day Inland Lake A Scow, one of the fastest monohull sailboats afloat. The plans for this monster (now at Mystic Seaport) may have excited one or two Fishers people, but they surely must have terrified a great many more because they went back to Mower and requested something a little more moderate.

Whether racing with spinnaker set or serving as a swimming platform in Hay Harbor, the 24-foot Fishers Island One Design—including the Morgan family's Bittern *(#8)—was the chief racing class at the Island from 1910 into the 1930s.*

Courtesy M. Lee Gaillard

He offered a 24-foot centerboard sloop with a draft, board up, of only 18 inches that allowed it to fit into Hay Harbor so long as it stayed away from the shoals. Many sisters and cousins of this boat were sailing on salt and fresh water across North America, from Brooklyn to Manitoba, under various names; sailboat racing then was a local sport with very few national or even regional classes. The Hay Harbor sailors called it Fishers Island One Design, or FIOD. The price from the Henry B. Nevins yard at City Island, New York, is not known, but a near-sistership sold for $400, the equivalent today of about $7,500.

Part of the excitement was dodging the shoals and rocks at Hay Harbor's tide-swept mouth on the way to or from the races. "Every foot forward over the bottom was a major victory," recalled Happy Gaillard. Courtesy M. Lee Gaillard

There seems to have been some concern that the new boat was unseaworthy due to its shallow draft and relatively short length. A press kit for the FIOD listed a number of safety devices, including interior lead ballast to improve stability, plus buoyancy tanks to keep the hull afloat should that not be enough lead to keep it from capsizing. The press kit also included a drawing that showed a boat that was at least 35 feet long. This could have been a mistake, but it also could have been a deception intended to assure the Hay Harbor sailors—who the release referred to as "members of the fashionable summer colony of Fisher's Island"—that they should have no worries. Eight members ordered boats, and in the summer of 1910 Walton Ferguson's *Christabel* steamed into Hay Harbor as escort for a tow of eight new Fishers Island One Designs, delivered the length of Long Island Sound. Two more FIODs arrived over the next few years.

Due to construction problems and uneven competition, in 1922 those ten boats were sold to the mainland and replaced by slightly altered, stronger, and more equal FIODs, still under gaff-headed rigs (in 1929 the class adapted the modern triangular Marconi rig). A copy of the contract for these boats between the Nevins yard and William D. Gaillard (Happy Gaillard's father) reveals a strong little yacht built of first-class materials. Blocks were brass, trim was mahogany, frames were white oak, planking was white cedar, and fastenings were bronze. One clause read, "The planking must be carefully planed, then caulked and puttied with white lead putty, then scraped and sandpapered until perfectly smooth to the complete satisfaction of the architect." You can almost smell the wood shavings. A new FIOD cost $985, or as much as three Ford Model-Ts. The main reason for the steep price was that the builder, Henry Nevins, demanded and got a

Sometimes a watchful eye was kept by a parent's yacht, like Walton Ferguson's Christabel. *The FIODs were later converted to the Marconi rig. They are now the A Class at Groton Long Point.* Courtesy M. Lee Gaillard

$500 profit. The sailing boom of the 1920s was a seller's market. As usual before World War II, the purchase price included everything that was needed to sail the boat, including sails, an anchor and rode, a brass bilge pump, a boat hook, three life preservers, oars for getting around in calms, and even a "fly at masthead" for finding the wind.

Sixteen of these second-generation FIODs came to Fishers in 1923. According to James F.X. Egan, the historian of the class (and its later incarnation as the Class As of Groton Long Point), the following were among the original owners of the 1923 boats: Henry Wilmerding, the Fulton family, George Watson, William Gaillard, William O. Morgan, two Ferguson families, Mortimer M. Buckner, Alfred W. Dater, Pip Sinclair, Thomas W. Russell, Rachel Porter, Charles S. King, and Blair S. Williams. Except for the Gaillards' *Swallow*, all the FIODs eventually changed hands at Fishers and were sailed by various du Ponts, Maxwells, and other families.

The last FIOD to leave Fishers was the Gaillard family's Swallow. *Still under her original name, she and nine other Class As were sailing at Groton Long Point in 2003, at least 93 years after Charles Mower drew their lines. They annually race over to Fishers where Happy Gaillard—pleased that the old boats are still doing so well—shuttles the sailors over to the Pequot Inn for lunch. "I am so glad they found such a good haven, even though I grieved at the time they left," Happy has written.*

The Fishers Island One Design has its quirks. The low boom, high centerboard trunk, and running backstays cause a tight squeeze for the crew when changing tacks. Downwind, the original spinnaker was flown entirely on the windward side of the headstay; jibing was a serious challenge. And the FIODs could and did capsize. Ed Maxwell and his brothers, the twins Bill and Dick (known as "Cooch"), won the season championship in 1930 and might have made it two straight in 1931 if Ed had not cleated the mainsheet. "An older fellow said they wouldn't flip," he explained.

As successful as the One Design was, its appeal faded in the early 1930s, when many of its sailors became interested in sailing more comfortable keel boats out of the Island's new sailing center on West Harbor's relatively deep waters. In 1933 most FIODs were sold to the mainland, where they ended up at Groton Long Point. For one season they sailed over to West Harbor to race against the remaining Fishers boats, but after the Groton Long Point Yacht Club was founded in 1934, they sailed off the Connecticut shore and were renamed Class As, because they got the first starting gun.

Swallow *beats to windward in light air, flying her racing flag.*
Courtesy M. Lee Gaillard

Cupid Takes a Back Seat

Old boats are rarely forgotten, and some are kept close in memory. Jim Egan, of Groton Long Point, has passed on this funny story about a Groton Long Point sailor:

Sometimes even Cupid took a back seat to the passion generated by these remarkable boats. Howard Dodd Jr. tells of sailing off toward Fishers Island in a Class A in the late '30s with a young lady aboard and romantic notions. They anchored in a cove on the north side of Fishers and dropped the sails. They were settling down for a picnic and a quiet afternoon when they heard a knock on the hull. They looked up and didn't see anyone. Looking over the side, they met a young swimmer who promptly climbed aboard. His family had owned this boat in the '20s. They spent the rest of the afternoon discussing the boats, the fleet, and sailing—subjects no doubt of compelling interest to Howard's nubile companion.

"A Whole Summer Lay Ahead"

After William Gaillard and his family started coming to Fishers in 1909, they fell into a routine that his daughter Marie, known as Happy, has recalled with affection. Even before she stepped off the ferry each June, she was swept up in anticipation of sailing and friends. "A whole summer lay ahead, endlessly full of happiness." Sailing on Hay Harbor brought community. Years later, standing outside her house, she inscribed Hay Harbor with a sweep of her arm, pointing out places where piers used to be. "See, the harbor was full of boats. Every house had a dock and every dock had at least one boat. There were motor yachts, sailboats, lots of canoes, rowboats, and Skiddoos."

At low tide, there was so little water that even a shoal-draft FIOD could run aground near shore, so *Swallow* was moored out in the harbor, where she served as the family's swim float. Sailing back from a race through the tight Hay Harbor entrance was challenging and, Happy recalled, occasionally romantic:

With the prevailing southwest wind, sailing into the channel, homeward bound, was always a challenge, especially with a strong ebb tide knocking the boat down with each tack so that every foot forward over the bottom was a major victory and a good lookout on the bow was invaluable. Once in a long while there would be enough breeze and enough moonlight for a night sail. Then the tack up-channel—it was rarely the reverse—was even trickier and the lanterns on the stakes, set out by the club launch at dusk, were reassuring guides.

William Gaillard and two of his children pose in the spacious cockpit of a catboat, their cottage prominent in the background.

Courtesy M. Lee Gaillard

The Hay Harbor Club gave way to the Fishers Island Yacht Club as the Island's sailing center.

Courtesy M. Lee Gaillard

Too Many Wrecks to Name

The names of several wrecked ships have become part of the Island's map and history. Isabella and Viking Beaches are named for the *Isabella Blake* and the *Viking*, which smashed up there in 1879 and 1925, and the old Fishers ferryboat *Olinda* was named for a Portuguese tramp steamer that grounded near West Harbor in 1895. But there have been too many wrecks at or near Fishers to be recorded in place names.

There is no Cochran Ledge, named for the carpet tycoon and yachtsman Alexander Smith Cochran, whose 282-foot steam yacht *Warrior* ran aground on Fishers in 1916 with her decks crowded with polo players. Race Point, likewise, is not called Morgan Point even though Commodore J.P. Morgan was lounging on the afterdeck of his chartered yacht at the start of the 1940 New York Yacht Club Cruise when her captain identified rocks in the Race the hard way (the yacht was eventually hauled off by a tug). Embarrassment reached a new level in 1912 when the schooner *Maggie Ellen* ran ashore on Fishers and was soon followed in exactly the same place by the *Estelle*, whose crew mistook the *Maggie Ellen*'s lights for Race Rock.

The wreck of the bootlegger *Thelma Phoebe* in April 1923 occasioned one of the more bizarre events in the Island's maritime history. A 157-ton former luxury yacht and World War I patrol boat, she was in service as a rumrunner, transporting illegal liquor during Prohibition, when she fetched up on a rock off Chocomount Beach. One crewmember died (his body, as was usual then, was stored in one of the Island's icehouses until it could be taken to the mainland), but what attracted the most attention was the ship's cargo. Soon after she grounded and opened up, cases and bags of Scotch whiskey began washing up on shore. Although it was only early spring, Chocomount Beach quickly became crowded with the Island's winter people. Robert G. Shanklin, the son of a Fishers Island official, later recalled the colorful scene in an article in the *New London Day*:

My excitement mounted as more arrived every minute until about 200 of the Island's 500 residents were milling around. Dozens of soldiers from Fort H.G. Wright added to the crowd, the largest gathering of people I had ever seen on the Island. The cases and bottles were disappearing as fast as they were being washed up. I saw many of our dignified neighbors helping to clear the beach of flotsam in a not so dignified manner, and soon only a few cases could be seen in the breakers.

As time passed, some of the people, no doubt stimulated by the spirit of adventure, went into the surf after the floating cases. To my delight one of our neighbors fell head over heels in the water trying to rescue a bag of Scotch. Much of the liquor was drunk on the spot and some people became unruly and noisy. The tide was ebbing and soon the vessel could be boarded with only wet feet. The lone guard, Elias W. Miner of the Coast Guard, tried to keep people away from the hulk, but only after firing two shots in the air did they obey his orders.

At least 1,500 of the 2,300 cases and bags went unaccounted for. "I was never to hear anyone on the Island say that he actually salvaged a bottle," Shanklin recalled, "but all the stories told about the episode ended in knowing smiles and winks."

Fishers Island's history of wrecks includes all types of vessels. (Above) *Viking Beach is named for the 48-foot schooner* Viking, *which was carrying potatoes when she ran into and eventually broke up on the south shore of Fishers in 1925.* Courtesy Helen Best

(Upper right) *The 282-foot steam yacht* Warrior *was on her way to a polo match when she ran up on the Island in 1916.* Courtesy Tom Armstrong

(Right) *After the bootlegger* Thelma Phoebe *smashed up on the Island in 1923, her cargo of whiskey quickly disappeared despite the efforts of the Coast Guard.* Courtesy Hedge family

The new club quickly adopted a burgee, or club flag, with a white diamond on a blue field–a design that suggests an island or a sail upon the sea.

One Boat per Member

The club was an immediate success, with 110 members from nine states and the District of Columbia in 1930. It also had 110 boats, including 23 Skiddoos (a press agent's dream). By comparison, in 2002, when the summer population was much larger, there were 313 senior members and 217 boats.

Here are some facts about the club in 1930:

110 Members – 66 senior members
44 junior members

110 Boats –6 Fishers Island One Designs
21 Bullseyes
23 Skiddoos
24 cruising sailboats
26 powerboats

Dues: Senior Membership, $20
Family Membership, $35
Jr. Membership (ages 10-16), $5
Associate Membership (non-boat owners), $5

Racing fees: FIS 31, $50
Schooner Class, $20
FIOD, $15
Bullseye, $10
Skiddoo, none

(To update 1930 dollars to 2004 dollars, multiply by 10)

The Fishers Island Yacht Club's first commodore, Arthur E. Whitney, sails aboard his Fishers Island Sound 31 Chance *in 1932. He led the club through its two greatest crises—the Great Depression and the 1938 hurricane.* Morris Rosenfeld photo. 1984.187.60668F, © Mystic Seaport, Rosenfeld Collection

The Second Yacht Club Is Founded, for Keeps

In 1928 some Fishers sailors and powerboaters who had stakes in the Island's future and boats too big to fit in Hay Harbor formed the West Harbor Yacht Club. A year later, they changed the name to Fishers Island Yacht Club. At the time of the most vigorous real-estate development in Fishers' history, this more straightforward and inclusive name enhanced the Island's image as a modern resort. The second club has been described as a "reorganization" of the club founded 42 years earlier by George Bartlett and his group. The truth, however, is that there was nothing left to reorganize. The second club was an altogether new institution. The only things it and the old club shared were a name and a connection with development at Fishers. The new club's certificate of incorporation, approved by a New York judge on July 19, 1934, was for a

(Right) Commodore Franklin M. Haines was so devoted to John Alden schooners that he owned three successive ones named Marita. (Above) Here is he at the left as his captain, Walter Bohlen, rows him out to the 46-footer Marita on her mooring with sails in stops ready to get underway. Courtesy W. Frank Bohlen

Fishers Island Yacht Club that had no plans for a presence anywhere but on the Island. Unlike the first club, then, the second one dedicated itself to providing services to people there, and that is why it immediately thrived and inevitably survived for more than three-quarters of a century.

The founding commodore of the second Fishers Island Yacht Club was Arthur E. Whitney, who raced a Fishers Island One Design and owned a powerboat and a cruising sloop. The club's only two-term commodore (he served in 1928-32 and 1937-38), Whitney presided when the club encountered the most challenging events in its history, the stock market crash and the 1938 hurricane.

Extremely unusual for a yacht club until relatively recently, the club's first rear commodore was a woman, Nancy Archibald Fuller (Mrs. Henry J. Fuller), a racing skipper. Although many women raced and cruised boats at that time, few clubs had female officers, much less allowed women members. Yet this new yacht club had six women members (almost 10 percent of the senior membership) and a female flag officer.

1930 Season Champions

Fishers Island One Design

1st – *Kite*, Edward Maxwell

2nd – *Sea Gull*, Mary Ferguson

3rd – *Swallow*, Gaillard family

Fishers Island Sound 31

1st – *Shanty*, Eben B. Knowlton

2nd – *Chance*, Arthur E. Whitney

3rd – *Canuck*, Mrs. Henry J. Fuller

Bullseye

1st – *no. 33*, Haines family

2nd – *no. 32*, Parsons family

3rd – *no. 25*, Bill Maxwell

Skiddoo

1st – Winthrop Haviland Jr.

2nd – Judith Russell

3rd – Peter Talbot

Schooner Handicap Class

July 4th Race, 1st – *Marita*, Franklin M. Haines

Labor Day Race, 1st – *Marita*, Franklin M. Haines

Run to Woods Hole, 1st – *Zingara*, Hollyday S. Meeds

From skiffs to sloops and catboats, West Harbor displays a variety of pleasure and working craft in this 1895 view. The Fishers Island Yacht Club eventually settled there on the west shore at a spot obscured by the sail of the middle catboat. James S. Casey photo. Henry L. Ferguson Museum

Changing Harbors

The most important influences on the formation of a new yacht club in West Harbor were the silting up of Hay Harbor and the simultaneous growth of interest in large boats that would not fit there. That the lagoon called Hay Harbor was getting shallower was beyond dispute. Reynolds du Pont was exaggerating only slightly when he remarked, "The anchorage will have to be moved soon before the bottom comes up to the surface with beer cans." A place that 20 years earlier had provided docks for large steam yachts was now having trouble with small boats.

Lammot du Pont's 97-foot motor yacht Marmot *lies at the wharf in West Harbor in August 1938, while the yacht club launch,* Active, *scurries by in the foreground as yachting expands in West Harbor.* Henry L. Ferguson Museum

One proposed solution was to dig a canal through Stony Beach to allow the full force of the tide to enter the harbor and scour its bottom. After some discussion, that costly option was rejected in favor of shifting the Island's yachting center altogether to West Harbor. There was a problem with depth there, too, with just 10 to 14 feet of water in the channel for the ferry and commercial and military vessels. When the Army, local businessmen, and fishermen successfully lobbied the government to widen and deepen the channel in 1930, West Harbor's future as a yachting center became brighter, although recurring problems with silting meant that it would have to be dredged again in the future.

By 1935 sailing at Fishers had a different look. Anybody standing on the porch of the seven-year-old Fishers Island Yacht Club's clubhouse would see a full yacht anchorage. Lying at moorings set out by a local fisherman, Skip Lawson, were four keelboat racing classes and an impressive fleet of cruising boats, including several deep-draft schooners, yawls, sloops, and powerboats as large as 140 feet. Over in Hay Harbor—which the new club listed as a station—there were only a couple of FIODs, the many little Skiddoos, and some shoal-keel Bullseyes (introduced in 1929). In 1939 the Bullseyes were shifted over to West Harbor, and the club was finally based in one port, except for the beginning sailors in the Dumplings, Weasels, and the Skiddoos' later successors at Hay Harbor.

One of the 12-inch coast artillery guns at Fort H.G. Wright hurls a shell seaward. Courtesy Harry Ferguson

A New Kind of Hazard

Storms and shipwreck presented enough problems for sailors in the Fishers region, but with the twentieth century came two new hazards. One was from below—the surfacing of submarines during trial runs out of Groton. The other, far more lethal threat came from above.

After Fort H.G. Wright was established in 1898 on the southwest shore of the Island as a base for the U.S. Army Coast Artillery Corps to guard the entrance to Long Island Sound, it was gradually outfitted with an ever-larger arsenal of ever-bigger guns. Before testing or target practice, soldiers usually cleared the area by sending out small boats to warn off nearby vessels. But the Army slipped up on August 13, 1925, when shells almost hit two sailboats. One came within 100 yards of clipping the schooner *Vagrant*, owned by former New York Yacht Club Commodore Harold S. Vanderbilt, and another five bracketed a small sloop, *Alouette*, the closest falling only 50 yards off her bow as the helpless sailors watched, terrified, until the firing was called off back at Fort Wright.

The queen of John Nicholas Brown's large fleet of boats of all sizes was his 91-foot Herreshoff schooner Saraband, *seen here blasting the tops off waves two years before the 1938 hurricane tore her up.* Morris Rosenfeld photo. 1984.187.77010F, © Mystic Seaport, Rosenfeld Collection

Another of Franklin Haines's *Maritas* was this handsome 58-footer of 1930, an Alden schooner as usual, seen charging along under her gollywobbler.

Morris Rosenfeld photo. 1984.187.46089F,

A Fleet of Schooners

Despite the gloomy economic climate, plenty of yachts were on display at Fishers throughout the 1930s. The glamorous sailboats were schooners, and the largest and most glamorous of them was *Saraband*, John Nicholas Brown's 91-footer from the great Herreshoff yard of Bristol, Rhode Island (like all Brown's yachts, named for a dance). Smaller at 64 feet, but still imposing, was *Barlovento*, owned by the yacht club's longtime commodore, Pierre S. "Pete" du Pont III. There were so many schooners around in the '30s that the handicap class, which raced on the annual cruise and national holidays, was often called "the schooner class."

The cruising boat that stirred the most hearts was C. Vaughan Ferguson's little John Alden-designed semifisherman schooner *Mary Leigh*, which, according to Dave Burnham, "looked so warm and friendly we thought of her as alive. My dad hungered for that boat." The work of Alden, a Boston designer who specialized in handsome, fast schooners with easy round lines reminiscent of classic fishermen, was well represented at Fishers. When three black Alden schooners named *Marita* were not under sail, they usually could be found moored east of Clay Point off the home of her owner, Franklin M. Haines. Come a

(Above) *Sailing formally and informally on board Commodore John Nicholas Brown's big schooner* Saraband. Courtesy Margaret Scott Ott

(Right) *One of the many larger boats demanding deeper water was Mortimer Buckner's 60-foot yawl* Pampero. *Like many yachts in the Fishers fleet she did not have an engine. Here she is two years before she was wrecked in the 1938 hurricane.* Morris Rosenfeld photo. 1984.187.77753F.

hard northerly, however, Captain Walter Bohlen (Frank Bohlen's father) would bring *Marita* around to West Harbor to find a more protected anchorage. Haines successfully raced *Marita*. In 1936 the 46-footer won a race around Cape Cod to Marblehead, beating several crack new sloops.

Besides taking a vigorous role at the yacht club—he headed the movement to acquire new sailboat classes for adults and children, including his own sons—Haines led the revival of the Island's golf club after it went bankrupt. Working closely with him there as well as on the water was another early commodore, Thomas W. Russell, (who for some reason was nicknamed "Whistlebritches"). After World War II, Russell remained influential, but Haines was less active due to family problems, including the death of his son George (known as Daud) in World War II when his ship sank and he gave his life preserver to a nonswimmer.

Like *Marita*, several boats were moored outside West Harbor. One was Irving W. Bonbright's yawl *Dartaway*, kept in Chocomount Cove off his big boathouse. Nearby lay one of Bonbright's powerboats, all named *Little Gull*, and Alfred Dater's little yawl *Altair*. One of the sleekest boats was Mortimer Buckner's 60-foot *Pampero*, a Herreshoff New York 40 racing sloop converted to the yawl rig. Strange as it may seem today, *Pampero*, like many larger boats built before World War II, did not have an engine, which was considered to spoil a good day afloat and detract from the rigors of able seamanship. Boats as large as 100 feet picked up moorings under sail even in crowded anchorages like West Harbor. Chris Roosevelt recalls watching his cousin George Emlen Roosevelt handle his engineless black schooner *Mistress*: "It was a wonderful sight to watch him coming into West Harbor to pick up his mooring, threading his way gracefully through the moored and anchored fleet in almost any wind, turning at just the right time to glide slowly up to his mooring and stall perfectly at the pick-up stake."

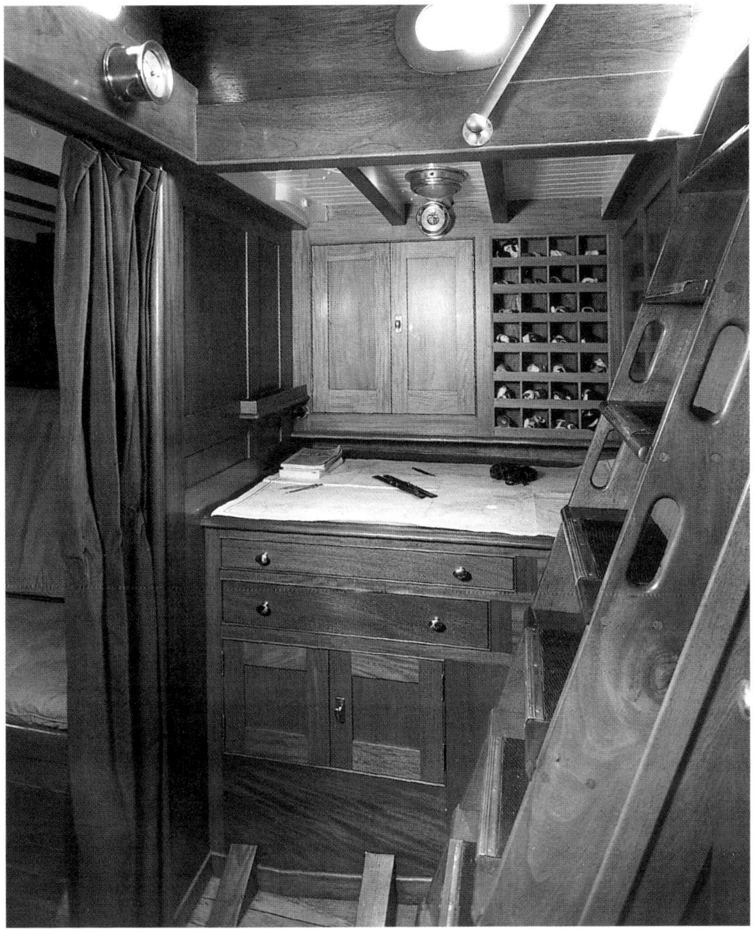

Barlovento

When Pierre S. du Pont III wanted an ocean-racing schooner, Cox & Stevens designed and the Pendleton yard of Wiscasset, Maine, built a 65-foot schooner that he named *Barlovento* when she took to the water in 1932. He and his family raced and cruised in her for more than a quarter century. Although du Pont built another big boat with the same name, the schooner is remembered at Fishers as "the" *Barlovento*.

(Opposite) *Still going strong at age 20,* Barlovento *charges down on the Rosenfeld camera.* Morris Rosenfeld photo. 1984.187.133045F, ©Mystic Seaport, Rosenfeld Collection

Barlovento had classic looks both above and below deck. (Left) *Here is her navigation station at the base of the main companionway. Before modern electronic charts, wide-ranging boats needed to store dozens of paper charts.* Morris Rosenfeld photo. 1984.187.42335, © Mystic Seaport, Rosenfeld Collection.

(Lower left) *And here is* Barlovento*'s saloon, looking aft toward the off-center companionway and the owner's stateroom.* Morris Rosenfeld photo. 1984.187.42337, © Mystic Seaport, Rosenfeld Collection

(Below) Barlovento *had a large, comfortable cockpit and a clean deck layout. Note the paucity of winches.* Morris Rosenfeld photo. 1984.187.42333, © Mystic Seaport, Rosenfeld Collection

The 150-foot diesel-powered Colleen, *which delivered Sir Samuel Salvage and his family on overnight runs to and from Fishers, was one of the old-style commuter boats—a luxuriously appointed floating mansion.* Morris Rosenfeld photo. 1984.187.32225, © Mystic Seaport, Rosenfeld Collection

The Commuters

In the early days of the yacht club, the Island had a fleet of large power yachts. The most conspicuous was *Oceania*, a steel 156-footer owned by Donaldson Brown, who served as treasurer at both DuPont and General Motors. This old-fashioned commuter boat, with an emphasis on luxury, not speed, brought her owner up from New York late in the week and lay at her mooring off Clay Point until Sunday evening, when Brown came aboard to be carried back to the city overnight. Only slightly smaller was *Colleen*, the 150-foot flagship of Sir Samuel Salvage, whose rayon empire, when teamed up with the du Pont interests, gave Fishers a near-monopoly on manufacturers of synthetics.

Here are some smaller commuters of the 1920s and '30s (from top to bottom): Stroller, *C.D. Rafferty's Herreshoff 46-footer* 1984.187.33746F © Mystic Seaport, Rosenfeld Collection; Avoca, *a 67-footer designed by Sparkman & Stephens and owned by E.E. Dickinson* 1984.187.92246F, © Mystic Seaport, Rosenfeld Collection; *and* Muskeeta, *designed by Alden, a more traditional 68-footer owned by Mrs. Howard F. Whitney.* 1984.187.19486F, © Mystic Seaport, Rosenfeld Collection

Smaller, quicker commuters included C.D. Rafferty's Herreshoff-designed and -built 46-footer *Stroller,* W.S. Carpenter's Consolidated 67-footer *Grey Gull* (with 1,200 horsepower in her twin engines), and the rockets that carried Everett Dickinson and his family between Essex and West Harbor—first *El Nido,* and later the 27-knot 67-footer *Avoca* (one of the last boats built at the Herreshoff yard). A somewhat more sedate representative of the new breed was Mrs. W. Shirley Fulton's *June XVI,* which David Burnham has described as "quite elegant as it headed out on a summer afternoon decorated with ladies in cardigans and straw hats."

Befitting an island, Fishers boasted a wide range of powerboats.
(Top) *H.B. Porter's* Sea Girl II, *a stylish runabout of the 1920s, ran the family in and out of Hay Harbor.* G.L. Thompson photo. Mystic Seaport 1980.156.195
(Below) *Sam Ferguson's* Escargot, *a Post yard "Sea Goin'" design, lies at her builder's yard on the Mystic River.* Mystic Seaport 1987.58.679

(Above) Mrs. W. Shirley Fulton's 47-foot June XVI, *designed by Kelley & Kyle, was at Fishers for more than 30 years. Here she flies the Fishers Island Yacht Club burgee as a spectator boat for the 1935 Harvard-Yale Race.* 1984.187.71512F, © Mystic Seaport, Rosenfeld Collection

(Left) The Hay Harbor Club launch, Sea King, was outfitted with awnings and wicker chairs for comfort while supervising races. 1987.58.763, © Mystic Seaport, Rosenfeld Collection

Almost from its founding, the Fishers Island Yacht Club has been based in this former Fort Wright ammunition shed. Here is how the clubhouse looked in the 1930s.

Adelard T. LeGere photo. Courtesy Sara Porter

"Simple Facilities for Yachtsmen"

Once the decision was made to relocate the club to West Harbor, the next question was where to put it. Consideration was given to a few places, including, reportedly, the Peninsula, the point jutting out into the harbor's south corner where the Burnhams spent their summers and several fishermen lived and kept their boats. But the officers settled on a site across West Harbor. Braced by a seawall of boulders, this spot of land had previously served as the foot of the Mansion House's impressive wharf. The club leased the land and marina from Fishers Island Farms, the Fergusons' management company—and also a shed said to have once been used to store ammunition at Fort Wright. That shed was still the clubhouse almost 75 years later.

The emphasis was not so much on buildings as on sailing. A promotional brochure for the Island got it right: "The Fishers Island Yacht Club provides simple facilities for yachtsmen, and also conducts a series of races and yachting events during the season." Almost all the club's resources went into boats. In 1935, for example, twice as much money was spent on racing prizes as on the clubhouse. Another year, the club spent more money on a racing buoy than on postage and printing. While the club regularly ran at a deficit, at a typical annual meeting members devoted much less time to discussing finances than to handing out trophies to race winners and debating class rules—for instance, whether Bullseyes should be allowed to fly genoa jibs.

This lack of interest in serious public discussion of the budget was an indication of security, not trouble. The shortfall was usually small enough to require no big sacrifice in a program that was already modest. When Reynolds du Pont, the club's longtime secretary-treasurer (and also a commodore), referred to "our customary austerity program," it was not without approval. He and most other members liked keeping things simple. The clubhouse was small, the marina was less than half the size of today's, there were no club-owned boats other than a couple of launches, and the junior sailing program consisted of one or two instructors who earned most of their pay in fees paid directly by parents.

Anyway, most of the membership did not have to worry about the deficit for the simple reason that it was not their burden. That duty was assumed by a few club officers, many of whom were wealthy and all of whom worried that hiking dues would scare away members. Among themselves they decided that the easiest solution to the deficit was simply to pick up the tab themselves. Besides cash, they provided the club with boats, moorings, furniture, new roofs, paint jobs, rebuilt launch engines, and much more. The ranks of these "good fairies," as Reyn du Pont called them, included flag officers, members of the board of governors, and their wives. John Nicholas Brown was a good fairy, and so were Reyn du Pont and his brother Pete. "Uncle Pete and Uncle Reyn kept the yacht club going," recalls Sandy Riegel, later a commodore himself. "Every time a financial problem appeared, they reached into their pockets and came up with a couple of hundred bucks." There would come a time in the 1950s when even fairy dust could not solve a financial problem, but usually the club got along very nicely under this paternalistic system.

The lively Maxwell crew aboard their Fishers Island Sound 31 Kelpie *during the 1933 Block Island Race. Left to right: Dick "Cooch" Maxwell, Jack Keeshan, Ned Anderson, Ed Maxwell at the helm, and Captain "Bill" Rathbun of Noank, whose main function was to keep the boys out of serious trouble.* Courtesy Maxwell family

Individualists

Much of the club's energy in its first 20 years went into choosing sailboat classes, several of which were commissioned for the club's own use. The amount of thought that went into this process is impressive. Each class was chosen for a particular use or age group, and most were so identified with the Island that, at one time or another in their history, they carried its name. The club's unwillingness to go along with everybody else was noted by the *The Rudder* magazine in 1939: "The Fishers Island Yacht Club have always been individualists to a great extent where their racing classes were concerned."

One thing that the new boats had in common was keels. The old Fishers Island One Design's history of capsizing was etched permanently in the club's memory. Twenty years after the FIODs left the Island, Reyn du Pont turned away a proposal for a new centerboard boat with a reference to "some fairly violent experiences in the past." Led by Commodores Frank Haines and Tom Russell, and other members, the club commis-

The Maxwells

An important part of sailing at Fishers to this day is the Maxwell clan. J. Rogers Maxwell began racing on New York Bay in the 1860s and owned big racing schooners, and his son, Henry L. Maxwell, a commodore of the Larchmont Yacht Club, began to come to Fishers Island in the 1920s with his sons Bill, Dick ("Cooch"), and Ed. Ed's son Wes is known to many Fishers sailors; his daughter Erin finished third in the 2003 women's 470-Class Olympic trials, won by Fishers Island Yacht Club's own Isabelle Kinsolving, sailing with Katie McDowell.

The three Maxwell brothers were fine sailors and exuberant, memorable characters. They raced around Hay Harbor in a small outboard powerboat named *Okham and Eggs*. Down at Larchmont, they figured out how to fire small projectiles out of the yacht club decorative cannon using cherry bombs as ammunition. This game ended after they finally succeeded in plugging a commodore in the back with a tennis ball.

Henry L. Maxwell's Fishers Island Sound 31 Kelpie, *sporting a fresh coat of red paint, emerges from the shop at the Herreshoff Manufacturing Company in the summer of 1930.*

Herreshoff Marine Museum

sioned or otherwise welcomed four new keelboat classes during the '30s, all of them admired for their graceful looks as well as their stability. (See Appendix 3 for a roster of Fishers Island classes.)

Three of these classes came from the country's (if not the world's) most respected yacht yard—The Herreshoff Manufacturing Company of Bristol, Rhode Island. Its boats won every America's Cup from 1893 to 1934—eight cup matches in all—and dominated almost every other racing event between 1890 and 1930. Many Herreshoff boats are still sailing today, including the Bullseye. Nathanael Greene Herreshoff and his brother John pioneered in modern design, in lightweight but strong wooden and metal construction, and in imaginative fittings. After Nat Herreshoff retired in the 1920s, his son Sidney produced three Herreshoff classes that were important at Fishers, two of them modifications of his father's designs.

The fleet of Fishers Island Sound 31s reaches out of West Harbor in the early 1930s. Nearest is #10, Elisha Cooper's Surprise. *The dark-hulled boat under spinnaker is the Maxwells'* Kelpie, *with North Dumpling off her bow.* Edwin Levick photo. Courtesy Maxwell family

The Fishers Island Sound 31

The first keelboat class at Fishers was the graceful Herreshoff-designed and -built Fishers Island Sound 31, or FIS-31. The number refers to waterline length, considered the best indicator of a boat's speed. The class originated with a sailor at Watch Hill Yacht Club, W. Barklie Henry, which explains its name referring to local waters. In the Herreshoff yard's promotional materials, however, "Sound" was deleted and the boats were called the "Fishers Island One Design." Obviously Fishers Island had a certain cachet among yachtsmen, or at least among yacht salesmen, for its name also was applied to two other boats, the Bullseye (called the "Fishers Island Bullseye") and the Herreshoff 23 (the "Fishers Island 23").

The FIS-31 is A. Sidney DeWolf Herreshoff's slightly larger version of one of his father's most successful pre-World War I boats, the Newport 29, one of which, the long-successful *Dolphin*, still sails in the Sound. Priced at $13,000 (the equivalent of about $130,000 today), the 31 was complete with everything needed to cruise, including china. By modern standards, accommodations are extremely skimpy, with only two cabins and a total of three bunks. This was a typical layout in a cruising boat of that era. The two bunks aft are for the owner's party, with their own enclosed head. Up in the bow was a tiny cabin, called the forepeak, with a single bunk and small toilet. That was the residence of the professional sailor in khaki uniform. He (it was always a he) scrubbed the decks, polished the brass, kept up the brightwork, washed the salt off all surfaces, and cooked the meals in a dark, narrow forward galley.

Beginning in 1929, six FIS-31s sailed out of Fishers Island: the Maxwell family's *Kelpie*, Elisha H. Cooper's *Surprise*, Arthur Whitney's *Chance*, Mrs. Henry J. Fuller's *Canuck*, Joseph H. Holmes's *Qutee*, Pierre S. du Pont III's *Aldebaran*, and Thomas W. Russell's *Savage* (now called *Torch* and on display at the Herreshoff Marine Museum). *Kelpie* was still raced hard after 50 years, and *Surprise* (renamed *Patapsco*) sailed around the world in the 1960s, reportedly with the loss only of a running backstay.

Like most sailboats of that era, the Fishers Island Sound 31s had heavy displacement and an immense mainsail and small jib, plus a small cruising interior laid out for a couple and a paid hand. Several of these boats have gone on to great things, including a circumnavigation. Here, the Maxwells' Kelpie *(#11) leads two others in a race.*

Morris Rosenfeld photo. Courtesy Maxwell family

The Herreshoff 23

In 1931, Fishers sailors were attracted to a new class that looked very different from the FIS-31 and almost all other American keel boats of the time, with their large sail plans, powerful lines, and wide after decks. So fine and graceful as to be dainty, the new boat was known as the Fishers Island 23 almost everywhere except, ironically, at Fishers Island itself, where sailors called it the Herreshoff 23 and H-23. In the spring of 1932, club members sailed the initial six H-23s down from Bristol to West Harbor.

For her design, Sidney Herreshoff borrowed the Scandinavian Square Meter concept of a long, narrow, relatively light-displacement boat with a small sail plan. Besides their sleek beauty, the H-23s were distinguished by their rainbow colors. At a time when most boats were painted white, black, or dark blue, the H-23s were boats of many hues. The class attracted the club's best sailors, including seven commodores. Though its ranks were depleted by the 1938 hurricane, the H-23 remained the yacht club's primary adult racing class into the late 1940s.

Designed for the club by Sidney Herreshoff along the lines of Scandinavian boats, the slim, light-displacement H-23s were raced at Fishers for many years. Padick *was raced by Everett E. Dickinson and after World War II had a second life as Eliot Porter's* Red Cap.

Morris Rosenfeld photo. 1984.187.69120F, © Mystic Seaport, Rosenfeld Collection

Tronda, *the first H-23, was owned by Francis W. Cole.*

1984.187.65274F, © Mystic Seaport, Rosenfeld Collection

Courtesy Sara Porter

75-cent Halyards, $3 Tows, and Other Reminders of Changed Times

The Mystic Shipyard in the 1920s began specializing in caring for pleasure boats. A promotional brochure made promises that indicate how industrialized the Mystic River was at that time: "No soot, no smoke; no factories within one mile. No sewage or oil drainage." Here are shipyard charges for caring for a Bullseye in 1937:

- New flag halyard, $.75
- Towboat between shipyard and Fishers, $3
- New hatch cover for locker under after seat, $3.75
- New main and jib sheets and halyards, $6.65
- Clean, thoroughly sand, and refinish mast and boom with two coats of varnish, $7.50
- Clean and thoroughly sand, apply two coats of paint to topsides and deck, one coat on the inside, two coats of varnish on all brightwork and two coats of paint on the bottom, $28. Above after taking all finish down to the wood, $50
- Inside winter storage, $20.80 (Mystic Shipyard's rates ran from $1.30 to $2.50 per foot for storage for the entire winter).

(Left) J. Carter Brown gets his wooden Bullseye Conga, set up in the 1940s. Brown Center, Brown University

(Right) Some Bullseyes race at Fishers Island in the 1930s just as they would for many decades. Courtesy Geddes Parsons

"The Bullseyes Have Survived"

The third Herreshoff boat at Fishers was the Bullseye, the backbone for the club's sailing program for more than 50 years since its arrival in 1929, and still an active class. A Marconi-rigged development of the gaff-headed, Herreshoff 12½ sloop introduced in 1914, the Bullseye has an overall length of 15 feet 8 inches. Although it is a keelboat, the draft is only 2½ feet, so it usually could be sailed in much of Hay Harbor during its decade there before the class was moved to West Harbor in 1939. Over the decades Bullseyes have taken many forms. They have been built of wood or fiberglass. Originally they had wide, open cockpits, but now they have cuddies. Some Bullseyes set overlapping jibs; others have small ones. Over the years they have been called by many names, including Fishers Island Bullseye, Long Island Bullseye, Bulls-Eye, Bulls Eye, Bull's Eye, and just plain Bullseye, which is the name used today.

In the *Fishers Island Gazette* in 1989, Peter Rugg took his readers on an off-season tour of Bullseye country: "Most are in the barn across the road from the American Legion, but others are in garages, yards, or Pirate's Cove. This may not seem very interesting until one considers that this same class of boats has been stored here every winter, and sailed here every summer, for 60 years.... They are not very pretty, not very fast, not very 'hot' in national sailing competition, and not very comfortable for racing or cruising, but the Bullseyes have survived while other classes have come and gone.... The Bullseye is just part of sailing at Fishers."

1937 Season Championships

Dumpling

1st – D. Slater

2nd – Walter B. Allen Jr.

Skiddoo

1st – Bray Dorrance

2nd – Henry du Pont

Bullseye

1st – N.S. Slater Jr.

2nd – Alexander Harvey

Best examination in racing rules – Alexander Harvey

L-16

1st – Charles Ferguson

2nd – H. Lee Ferguson

H-23

1st – Franklin M. Haines

2nd – William H. Hubbard

Handicap Division

Cruise Class A –

Tie: C.A. Goodwin and Franklin M. Haines

Cruise Class B – E.E. Dickinson

The boat now known as the Luders 16 was yet another class designed for the Fishers Island club, in its case as a boat for teenagers. It was a popular class at Fishers Island until the 1938 hurricane devastated the fleet. (Above) *Luders 16 #1,* Bad Wolf, *shows her style soon after the class was introduced in 1934. She is flying a light reaching jib with her working jib doused on the foredeck.*

1984.187.69116F © Mystic Seaport, Rosenfeld Collection

(Right) *This photograph taken during early trials off the builder's yard emphasizes the L-16's sweet sheer and long, fine ends.* Mystic Seaport 1983.6.71

The Luders 16

During the Great Depression, the yacht club's membership declined precipitously to less than 80, yet sailing still remained strong with six classes and about 40 boats signed up annually for racing. The Skiddoos and, later, the Dumplings took care of the youngest sailors, while Bullseyes were raced by 15- and 16-year-olds. The H-23s were the major class for older adolescents and adults, and the few remaining FIODs still had starts until the Gaillards' *Swallow* was sold off the Island in 1937. The largest boats, the Fishers Island Sound 31s, continued to race and cruise out of the club and up and down Long Island Sound and southern New England.

In 1934 the club got its sixth class, which was aimed specifically at older teenagers. Sometimes called the Fishers Island One Design, it was usually referred to by the name of its designer-builder and its waterline length—Luders 16, abbreviated L-16. Twenty-six feet in overall length, it was created specifically for the club by the Luders Marine Construction Company in a competition run by a club committee headed by Frank Haines. Like most classes at Fishers, the L-16 had a sweeping, graceful appearance. With her extreme overhangs totaling ten feet, narrow beam of five feet nine inches, and heavy displacement of 3,200 pounds, the boat looked like a scaled-down version of the glamorous 36-foot Six Meter that was the hot international racing class. To a modern eye, the L-16 may look far too stately for today's junior sailors, who tend to be less interested in classic looks than high performance. Back then, however, the builders wanted "something get-

Reynolds du Pont and Geddes Parsons race du Pont's L-16 Port *at Fishers in the 1930s.*
Courtesy Geddes Parsons

ting away from the chunky little boats juniors usually sail," as Robert N. Bavier Jr. wrote in *Yachting* magazine. To put it another way, the goal was to have a kids' class that looked like a sleek adult yacht, not like the stubby little Bullseye or Skiddoo. Half a century later, the same standard governed the choice of another un-Bullseye at the Fishers Island Yacht Club, the International One Design, which also was modeled on the Six Meter.

On the last day of the 1934 American Yacht Club Cruise, several new Luders 16s sailed over to Clinton, Connecticut, to race in the 26-mile leg to West Harbor. Two were sailed by youngsters—*Marlin* by Frank Haines's sons, George and Daud, *Home Run* with Algie Ferguson at the helm and his cousin Charlie trimming sheets. Their competition was very grand indeed: 39 boats headed by three huge 80-foot M Class racing sloops and including some top ocean racers, including *Stormy Weather* and *Edlu*. The big fellows leapt out as expected at the start and were soon well over the limited horizon of the L-16 sailors. The first boat to finish, in 4 hours, 35 minutes, was the M-boat *Istalena*. Three hours later, long after they had put the covers on the sails and commenced celebrating their apparent victory, the crew looked up to see *Home Run* and *Marlin* bow to bow, *Home Run* winning by two seconds. Not until well after the race did both crews realize that though the huge *Istalena* had finished more than three hours earlier, they had beaten her by 12 minutes on corrected time to win the race.

When they were not raced hard by their young crews on Wednesdays and Saturdays, the L-16s spent many days on long sails on Fishers Island Sound or around the Island. Sometimes there were short cruises to neighboring waters until the 1938 hurricane turned most L-16s into kindling. Years later the Island resumed its relationship with the Luders yard when Pete and Reyn du Pont commissioned the 12-Metre *American Eagle*, which came close to winning the 1964 America's Cup defense trials and went on to a successful ocean racing career under Ted Turner and Warren Brown.

"I Loved the Racing"

There was lots of racing, and in those days almost all of it took place in local waters. Long before there were regional junior championships, the Parsons Trophy team races, and the busy Off Soundings Club racing schedule, before World War II, most sailboat racing took place within the club, with the exception of the occasional interclub team race with visiting sailors from Larchmont Yacht Club or Stonington's Wadawanuck Club.

Surviving race results from Wednesday and Saturday races in the 1930s, neatly written up in 12 notebooks now in the Henry L. Ferguson Museum, reveal that about two dozen boats with crews of adults or older adolescents usually raced on a summer Saturday, while about ten junior crews would be out on a Wednesday. H-23 and L-16 races were 6 to 9 miles long, and Bullseye races usually 4 miles, except on Independence Day and Labor Day when they might be stretched to 7 miles. The courses were usually around government marks or islets, like Seaflower. Unlike today, when sailors expect to start upwind and sail beats and runs aligned perfectly to the wind, in those days many races were started downwind, and a long reach was considered a desirable leg of the course. The scoring system used in monthly and season series encouraged participation. While a first place always got 100 points, the points for second place varied with the turnout: 75 points in a four-boat race, 90 points when there were 10 boats, and 93 points when there were 15 boats, with a sliding scale all the way down to last place. To win a season prize, you had to beat lots of boats regularly.

The Bullseye, L-16, and, later, the Quincy Adams 17 classes provided a natural ladder out of the Skiddoos for boys and girls who liked sailing and wanted to go beyond the basics. Instruction was by private tutors hired by parents, with the occasional specialist retained to teach one class or another.

Judging from the range of memories, the sailing program succeeded in offering all things to all people. Jean McIntire Leuchtenburg, like all young sailors at Fishers then, learned how to sail in Skiddoos from tutors hired by her parents. Her instructors were Geddes Parsons and Petey Talbot. She just sailed faster

FISHERS ISLAND HAS A HOLIDAY REGATTA

Many Families Opening Their Cottages for the Summer—Dance at Mansion House

Special to THE NEW YORK TIMES.

FISHERS ISLAND, N. Y., July 3. —The Fishers Island Yacht Club will hold a special regatta tomorrow, with trophies, donated by the club, for the winners in the three classes of regular yachts, H-23 footers, L-16 footers and bullseye. There will be an extra race for yawls, schooners and auxiliaries. The first Saturday regatta in the July championship series was held this afternoon.

The Hay Harbor Club held the first in its series of Saturday buffet luncheons this afternoon on the club porch.

The first dance of the season for the younger set will take place at the Mansion House here Tuesday.

A large crowd arrived yesterday for the week-end, which opens the Summer season here. The opening of the week-end also found a large number of families arriving at the cottages for the Summer and many guests at the Mansion House for indefinite stays.

Recent cottage arrivals are Mr. and Mrs. Theodore P. Grosvenor and family, who have taken the C. H. Goodwin cottage for the Summer, and Mr. and Mrs. Martin Saportas and family, who are at the Studio Cottage. Mr. and Mrs. Winslow M. Lovejoy are at the Glazier Cottage for the Summer. Mr. and Mrs. William H. Hubbard and daughter, Elizabeth, have returned to their Mansion House cottage for the Summer. Mr. and Mrs. Alfred R. Riggs are at the Prescott Cottage for the Summer and Mr. and Mrs. Thomas W. Russell and family have returned to their Summer home Windswept here.

Other arrivals were Mr. and Mrs. C. Bruce Campbell, Mr. and Mrs. Jansen Noyes, Mrs. Harold R. Talbot, Mr. and Mrs. C. D. Rafferty, Mr. and Mrs. Charles S. Campbell, Mr. and Mrs. John Nicholas Brown, Miss Charlotte Roberts, Mrs. R. E. Lee Taylor, Mrs. Beverly Ober and Mr. and Mrs. Orland S. Greene.

New York Times, July 1937.

"I loved the racing," recalled Jean McIntire (Leuchtenburg), here seen aft as Anne Campbell (Clement) rigs the jib on the Bullseye Buddy *in 1939. Cuddy cabins did not appear until Bullseyes were built of fiberglass after World War II.* Courtesy Jean McIntire Leuchtenburg

than most. In 1939, like other girls her age, she moved on to the Bullseye and commenced to clean up. From late June to late September, racing twice weekly in the green-hulled *Buddy* against a dozen or so competitors sailed by boys or girls named Parsons, Ferguson, and Dorrance (whom she remembered as "the Campbell's Soup boys"), Jean was queen of the Bullseyes. "I *loved* the racing. I don't remember reading technical articles on racing in *Yachting* magazine, though I did enjoy talking with people about how to make the best of the tide and understand the effect of the shore. It was a beautiful place to sail because it was such interesting water."

One of the highlights of the summer was the yacht club cruise to Shelter Island, Montauk, Saybrook, or up the Connecticut River to Essex. These were warm, inclusive affairs. The fleets of boats were large enough to provide a sense of spectacle, but intimate enough so everybody could eat under one roof, either ashore or in one of the big yachts, like Sir Samuel Salvage's 150-footer *Colleen*. During one of these cruises, Talcott Stanley and Charlie Ferguson were putting their L-16 *Black Duck* away when the launch pulled up with an urgent message from Fishers: "Don't light your kerosene lantern. Your father thinks that he might have filled it with gasoline!" The boys took a deep sniff and to their relief discovered that, this time at least, their parents were wrong. That was hardly the boys' first cruise, for they overnighted often in Fishers Island Sound. As Stanley and Ferguson recalled, "In the 1930s, a big adventure was to cruise the Bullseyes to Ram Island for the night and cook on a Sterno stove and eat sardines and marshmallows. It was a getaway." These voyages, of course, saw their share of high jinks. A firecracker somehow found its way into the water near the bow of a wooden Bullseye that, fortunately, had buoyancy tanks that kept her afloat until she could be hauled and recaulked.

"Lots of fun. No sleep," Harris Parsons says of those Ram Island cruises of long ago. "We always stayed in the boats overnight. Sleeping on an L-16 was real fun"–even (or especially) if there was little or no sleep to get.

Squalls and Other Troubles

The racing was not always placid, in large part because of the changeable summer weather. Nobody seems to have worried much about sailing in fresh winds. There was, for example, a 30-knot northwester at the 1931 Labor Day race, yet 27 boats started. Talcott Stanley recalled a wild August race at the helm of Mary Russell's H-23 *Quinta* when a sudden squall came up. "We were on a course between the Dumplings, and the following wind was not too strong. We decided to drop the jib and continue on. As we went through the Dumplings the squall hit us with rain, lightning, and hail. It only hailed a few minutes, but it was quite an experience to see the cockpit full of hailstones."

Charlie Ferguson, referring to himself by his initials, passed on a story of a hair-raising Bullseye Fourth of July race in the 1930s. "A black squall struck the fleet as they were off Clay Point headed for the finish line. C.B.F. and Walter Rafferty (the last time he was ever in a sailboat) lowered the sails, finished the race under bare poles, and beached the Bullseye at Grey Gulls." Harris Parsons recalled that same squall: "It was a Fourth of July race, my first race in a Bullseye, and we were on the last leg of the race when a bad squall came up and all the boats ended up at Walter S. Carpenter's dock at Grey Gulls except for Chas Cole, who had his collie dog as crew and his boat sank off Flat Hammock. Chas had one life jacket, which he put on the dog. They were soon picked up by the race committee."

Competition was known to be intense. One skipper, who wishes to remain anonymous, has confessed to whacking her crew over the head with a boom crutch when an order was not promptly obeyed. During a hard-fought Labor Day race, Eliot Porter was spilled overboard from Charlie Ferguson's Bullseye, yet the other boats kept on racing (fortunately, Porter grabbed a line and hauled himself back aboard). In another race, a crew charging along under spinnaker somehow failed to notice a rowboat and cut clean through it, fortunately slowing sufficiently so the fisherman could leap aboard.

Popular sailing instructor Art Lane explains the basics of a Skiddoo at Hay Harbor, around 1938.

Courtesy Marjorie Scott Ott

"The gray boat of the amazing, one-armed Ed Hedge," the Bessie H. Courtesy Hedge family

"A Boy's Eye View of West Harbor"

As a lad looking out from the family house on the Peninsula in the late 1930s, David Burnham (the second son of Rufus Bradford Burnham, who had found "perfect quiet" at Fishers) had a close view of West Harbor, with its colorful blend of fishing and pleasure boats small and large. Because the cottage was not wired for electricity, on many days he rowed across to the gas dock to buy kerosene. Sometimes he rowed across Fishers Island Sound to visit friends at Noank. Here is a portion of his memoir, "A Boy's Eye View of West Harbor."

I grew up in the 1930s and '40s as a summer child on the Peninsula, that special piece of land which juts into West Harbor, Fishers Island. On the east side of the Peninsula is Darby's Cove, navigable only by small powerboats and rowboats. On the west is the inner harbor guarded by Goose Island. Due north of the Peninsula is the real harbor. Looking northwest I could see the yacht club, and then slowly moving my eye clockwise I could see the Mobil Dock, the Mansion House Dock where the ferry came in, then Hawk's Nest Point, open water beyond the harbor flasher as we looked toward Noank and Ram Island, and then, to the northeast, Clay Point.

This was my territory. Add to it the inner harbor looking across to Murphys' with the Bonnell House a little to the left of it. Then came Joe Pavao's lobster dock and the Voorhis house. A little farther south were the Hedge and the Peishoff houses and the Roberts summer cottage. I ruled and I rowed over this territory. It was my kingdom whether I leaped from rock to rock along the shore or surveyed my land from a rowboat. Some of the rocks even had names. I could show you to this day "Old Fort Si" in front of our house or help you navigate the inside passage among the rocks north of Goose Island.

It was not just the sights which were important, but also the sounds of my watery realm. One would lie in bed in the attic of our cottage and tell which lobster boat was going out, whether it was the large green Pavao boat, Johnny Peishoff's brown boat, the gray boat of the amazing, one-armed Ed Hedge, or the noisy one-lungers of Gurd Hewlett or Joe Roderick. Later in the day one might see Mr. Roberts with his white round canvas hat steering his putt-putting launch, Delphine, *with a party of ladies on board, out through the Goose Island channel.*

Another sound would be that of sails hauled up to dry. Canvas sails had to be dried carefully to avoid mildew. In the morning one could hear the winches on the bigger boats as the sails went up and for an hour or two the flapping in the light morning breeze would be a familiar sound. So would be the whistle of the ferry Fishers Island *announcing its arrival as it came around Hawk's Nest Point. On crowded summer weekends there might be indignant hooting all the way to the dock while visiting boats which had quite innocently anchored in its channel scurried to get out of the monster's way.*

Dave Burnham in David Dorrance's Bullseye Wasp, *1941, sailing on West Harbor.* Courtesy Dave Burnham

"There will be Yachting"
The Challenges of Storm, War and Revival, 1938-1970

As the Great Depression weakened, the club recovered and in 1937 saw new highs of 112 members, with 44 boats racing five classes. There was so much activity that at the annual meeting someone proposed providing illumination on the landing float and asking the Coast Guard to patrol the race course.

The good times continued into 1938. That summer, 15-year-old Eliot Porter won most of the junior Bullseye trophies in *Viking*, while his younger sister, Maxine, took two cups in the Skiddoos. After the boats were towed to their winter home at Mystic Shipyard, and the champions returned to theirs in New Britain, Connecticut, their proud father, Maxwell S. Porter, passed the results on to the local newspaper, which published a nice little article about them.

(Left) Three generations of du Ponts cruise up the Mystic River on the Maid of Honor, *a former British Admiralty launch.* Mystic Seaport 1968-9-38A

(Above) Eliot Porter and his crew sail Porter's Bullseye Viking *in 1937, the year before her best season yet and the big hurricane.* Courtesy Sara Porter

The bubble was burst 11 days later by a telegram from Mystic Shipyard that read: "Your boat damaged in hurricane. Unable to determine extent up to now. Details will follow. Suggest advising your insurance agent of loss." *Viking*, in fact, was not insured. After Mr. Porter asked the yard for advice as to what he should do with his son's little yacht, the yard replied with a terseness that cuts to the quick of the disaster that was the 1938 hurricane. The manager promised that Mr. Porter would receive a report on the exact condition of the boat "just as soon as we are able to locate and examine it." Like almost every other

After Barlovento *dragged onto Hawk's Nest Point during the 1938 hurricane, she was floated free without significant damage.*

Courtesy Bradford Burnham Jr.

waterfront property in New England in late September 1938, Mystic Shipyard was a heap of splinters.

Around lunch time on a gusty Wednesday, September 21, 13-year-old Jean McIntire and her family were in their house near Chocomount Cove watching a continuous wave of water pour over the seawall, carrying seaweed so thick it caulked the house against the storm surge. When a long-buried wreck was lifted out of the beach and tossed—stern, keel, and all—over the seawall, the family decided it was time to get into the Packard and head to the hills on the west end of the Island. After barely avoiding the roof of John Nicholas Brown's new house, Windshield, lying in the road, they encountered Henry Lee Ferguson, who stepped out of a mess of fallen trees and guided them to his home. There they rode out "the Long Island Express," as the 1938 hurricane was called because it had roared in from Montauk.

One historian, Everett S. Allen, has called it "The greatest disaster in the history of eastern Connecticut." Any storm that (as a Vermonter living near the Canadian border once told this author) caused a house to "seem to swell and contract, just like a person breathing" is bound to inspire claims that Almighty God has brought vengeance on an evil world. That apocalyptic interpretation was disputed by The Rev. Arthur Lee Kinsolving, a summer rector at Fishers Island's St. John's Church. "There is no valid evidence that Christianity ever assumed the world would provide maximum security and comfort," he told his parishioners in Boston.

Of course, Kinsolving was far from the low, exposed Island as the 100-mile-an-hour wind blew down the St. John's steeple, scattered chimney bricks for miles, and caused other serious damage. A wave so high it looked like a fog bank cut Fishers in three, scoured Wicopesset Island clean of soil, wiped every house from off Watch Hill's Napatree Point, shifted the foundation under Latimer Reef light, and (curving around the Island's ends) swept into Hay Harbor to lift the Mononotto Inn's bathhouses and docks clean off their supports and carry them back into the Sound. "The beach used to be white, a nice beach," John Arasimowicz, a long-time Island man (known as Johnny Chestnut), recalled years later, "but over the years these storms changed all that."

Over in New London, the lighthouse tender *Tulip* went ashore with its bow on the railroad tracks near the train station. When the five-masted school ship *Marsala* smashed ashore into a warehouse complex, a short circuit started a fire that destroyed much of the town's business district. The *New London Day*'s headline the next day ran, simply, "City Ruined."

"Went ashore, some to eternity," Arthur Whitney said of the club's fleet. (Top to bottom) *Alfred Ferguson's powerboat* Hawk *nose-down at the gas dock, Charlie Ferguson's L-16* Home Run *blown over the seawall, and many missing roofs and foundered yachts.* Courtesy Bradford Burnham Jr.

The storm that almost destroyed New London could also have destroyed sailing at Fishers. If it had blown in three weeks earlier, or if the yacht club membership had not been as resilient as it was, the place might have taken many years to recover. The clubhouse escaped relatively unscathed, with only the spreader of the toppled flag pole sticking down into the roof. The club's pier and bulkhead were completely submerged, its float was in the road, and Alfred Ferguson's swordfisherman *Hawk* was hanging precariously from the gas station wharf. Of the other 53 boats in the club's fleet, some had been caught at their moorings, and many others at shipyards. The second group suffered the most damage. Thirteen boats (mostly Bullseyes and L-16s) were total wrecks. Only 17 boats went undamaged, although that word took on a new meaning at a time when the label "damage not serious" was applied to boats that had been stripped of all their spars and rigging. *Barlovento* was high and dry near Hawk's Nest Point. Not as lucky was *Saraband*, which was so beaten up in her slip at Newport that John Nicholas Brown declined to even attempt to bring her back; the great schooner ended her days as a houseboat on the Thames River.

The catastrophe was so great that people were left searching for appropriate language to describe it. One lost boat was described in words borrowed from the country's most popular book, "gone with the wind, not a trace left." Other boats, Commodore Arthur Whitney reported to the members, "went ashore, some to eternity." Most people, however, were unable to do better than a single pithy word. Charlie Ferguson described the fate of his L-16 very simply: "pulverized."

The cleanup after the 1938 hurricane included extracting George Porter's fishing boat Mononotto *from the brush and flotsam around Hay Harbor.*
Mystic Seaport 1989.116.51

At the end of his report of the devastation, Commodore Whitney did his best to be upbeat: "It is too early to say just now what recommendations will be made for the class racing, but your present, past, and future officers"—everyone, in other words—"are seriously at work on the subject. One thing you can depend on, there will be yachting, 'as usual,' at Fishers Island next summer." Others were not so sanguine. When Mystic Shipyard finally dug the remains of Eliot Porter's *Viking* out of the debris, the only things of value that remained nearly whole were the dented lead keel and some hardware.

After selling her for $40 to a fellow who hoped to rebuild poor *Viking* with another rig, Mr. Porter instructed the shipyard to find a Bullseye sailor who might be in the market for a suit of championship racing sails. In reply, the yard manager gloomily advised that it was hopeless to find such a buyer, at least at Fishers Island, where (he promised Maxwell Porter) the Bullseye class had been killed off forever.

The Quincy Adams 17

For anybody viewing the wreckage on Fishers, the only good news was that the seeds blown in by the hurricane would restore the Island's vegetation to a state of lushness not seen since the Island's last great storm, in 1815. But hope for happier summers revived as a few small boats were plucked off the shore with little damage, and as Pete du Pont liberated *Barlovento* from Hawk's Nest Point by digging a trench around her and, come high tide, pulling the schooner into it.

Most recovery was much slower. Twenty-two boats had raced out of West Harbor on Labor Day 1938; a year later, only 15 boats started the Labor Day race. The Bullseyes' Labor Day turnout was halved from eight to four, while the L-16 fleet almost disappeared, dropping from eight boats to three. The Bullseyes recovered quickly as builders turned out new boats; nine were sailing at Fishers in 1940. But the few remaining L-16s were soon sold to the mainland as the new Quincy Adams 17 was introduced for older teenagers.

The QA marked the end of an old, expansive era when, despite the depression, Fishers seemed unable to stop acquiring new classes. The last new keel-boat class until the arrival of the International One Design more than 40 years later, the QA served its teenage sailors happily into the 1960s. "The QA was a beautiful boat, more boat than the Luders," recalls Jean McIntire Leuchtenburg. Deriving its name from its builder, the Quincy Adams Shipyard in Massachusetts, the QA was drawn up by a New England designer and boating writer, Fred W. Goeller, with a more solidly traditional look than the racy L-16's. She also sailed better and faster, and offered more room for sailing and the other

Though not designed for Fishers Island, the Quincy Adams 17-footer was very well suited to succeed the L-16s as the boat for the Island's older junior sailors after the 1938 hurricane. There were QA-17s sailing at the Island for almost 30 years. Courtesy M. Lee Gaillard

A jaunty QA-17 sails through the anchorage in the outer part of West Harbor under the old cotton sails. Mystic Seaport 1952-9-3B

activities that interest adolescent crews. "It was a different kind of racing in QAs," Libbie Hubbard Cook remembers. "It was much more informal. We all took it pretty casually. For instance, the trophy never was engraved with the name of the last winner."

Nick Brown, a son of Commodore John Nicholas Brown, reminisced about these languid days of nautical hanging out:

I did quite a bit of daysailing. Clearly the strong tides and plethora of rocks developed a sense of seamanship absent, perhaps, in more benign waters. We especially loved to go round the Island—race or no. I really feel that the yacht club made an outstandingly positive imprint on all the sailors, especially those my age. We were conscious that lots of our friends were off playing golf and tennis, but we just liked to hang out along the docks. And we also learned that the girls loved to go sailing! I had a girl in Watch Hill but never could get into Little Narragansett Bay, so we would meet at Noank at Skipper's Dock.

Nick Brown learned two valuable lessons about boats from his years in the QA. One was that winning races demands assiduous attention to detail. That discovery helped him take many QA season championships against young Pete du Pont, Brad Middlebrook, Lew Thatcher, and other talented skippers. (Middlebrook, with Brown crewing, qualified to represent Fishers Island Yacht Club in the national junior sailing championship for the Sears Cup.)

The second lesson that Nick learned about the QA had nothing to do with racing: "I further discovered that the boat in the evening was a great place to take a date! In fact, one can cuddle nicely on a bagged spinnaker." Which goes to show that for sailors of a certain age, a boat's success may have less to do with yacht design than hormones.

(Above left) *Aptly named for the fleet-footed huntress of Greek mythology, the QA-17* Atalanta *was sailed swiftly by two of the Island's best sailors, her owner Elizabeth "Libbie" Hubbard (Cook), at the helm, and Maxine "Mocks" Porter (Arnold). Here they are during the club's 1946 cruise to Montauk.*

(Above right) *Libbie Hubbard and Bruce May make lunch while* Atalanta *is towed back to Fishers from Montauk.*

(Left) *After graduating from the QAs, many sailors moved into H-23s. Here, Eliot Porter and crew prepare* Red Cap. Courtesy Sara Porter

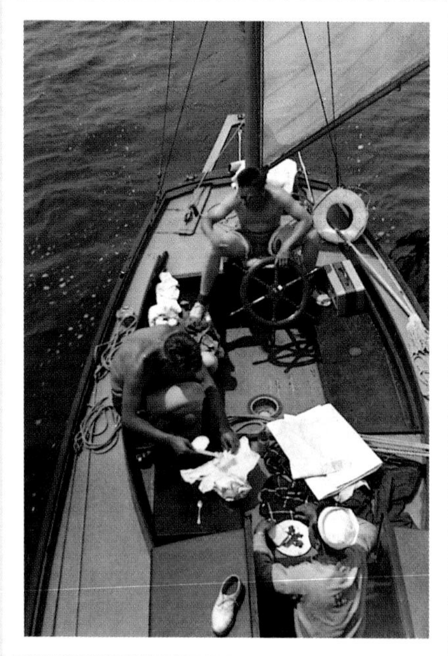

One of the fallouts of the 1938 hurricane was that while the Island lost many boats, it gained at least one. A small yawl called *Sparrow Hawk*, with a crew of Princeton undergraduates, was blown over South Beach, skipped along almost a quarter mile, and finally came to rest near the Parade Ground at Fort Wright. The crew survived in one piece, but the same could not be said for the vessel. Lee Ferguson and Lewis Lamb acquired *Sparrow Hawk* for $75 and put her back together again. The next summer, Lee's brother Charlie and two Williams College classmates cruised in her down Long Island Sound to the New York World's Fair.

Charlie Ferguson (in hat, pipe, and glasses) and some college friends sailed the restored Sparrow Hawk *down to the New York World's Fair in 1939 and, as their photos show, had a ball.* Courtesy Charlie Ferguson

The Rhodes 27

Sometime before the hurricane, several members were discussing the creation of a new club-endorsed cruiser-racer. When the committee could not agree on accommodations, two men went to Philip L. Rhodes, one of the most successful young American naval architects, for a new design. He submitted plans for a 39-foot sloop he called the "Fishers Island Class," making this the seventh class to carry the Island's name; the class was eventually renamed the Rhodes 27. She was meant to sail fast and also cruise comfortably. The interior was more commodious than the Fishers Island 31's, and more democratic, too. Now the cook stood in the well-lighted galley. After the boats came out of the Nevins yard at City Island at a price with sails of $7,500 (about $92,000 today), Phil Rhodes confided that this was his favorite design.

The first two Rhodes 27s were built for incoming Commodore Thomas W. Russell and his successor, William H. Hubbard, both of whom had lost H-23s in the hurricane. Russell's *Savage* almost did not make it out of the Nevins yard due to a miscalculation by her first paid hand, Brad Burnham Jr. Unfamiliar with the workings of an alcohol stove, he succeeded in setting the galley on fire. "I awaited the arrival of Mr. Russell with some trepidation," Burnham admitted many years later. "I am not sure that he ever realized how close he came to not having his dream boat, because when he arrived I had already obtained the services of a sympathetic painter in the yard who had the area sanded and half painted." The boat survived, as did Brad's career as a boat boy for a generous and loyal man who overpaid both Brad and his brother, David, to help with their college expenses. Another bonus followed the boat. Everett Dickinson, who had purchased *Savage* from Russell, put a provision in his will that gave Brad Burnham first refusal to acquire *Savage* for $25,000. "I was unable to do that in the end, but I did have a well-known, respected surveyor check her out, and he found her in amazingly good shape, recommending only that two ribs be sistered. She had been lovingly maintained every year of her life by the Mystic Shipyard."

Commodore Thomas W. Russell sails his beloved Rhodes 27 Savage, *another fine boat designed for Fishers Island sailors.* Courtesy David Burnham

R27
I
R27
I

(Left) *Showing off her functional doghouse and her classic Rhodes bow,* Savage, *with owner Thomas W. Russell in checked shirt, clips along one day in the early 1950s.* Morris Rosenfeld photo. 1984.187.123346F © Mystic Seaport, Rosenfeld Collection

(Right) *R-27 #2, William Hubbard's* Fairway, *powers along off Greenport during the 1941 Off Soundings Club races.* Morris Rosenfeld photo. 1984.187.100996F, © Mystic Seaport, Rosenfeld Collection

(Above) *Bill Hubbard sailed a Bullseye and an H-23 before building* Fairway*—whose name commemorated his passion for golf.* Courtesy Cook family

His Favorite Place

Here is how David Burnham has described the day's routine in the Rhodes 27 *Savage* (inspired by a family nickname for Russell's rambunctious daughter, Dolly) when he was her paid hand after World War II.

My routine was to use the morning dew to mop the decks and chamois the brightwork. If the boat had been sailed the day before, I went along the topsides in the pram with a bucket of fresh water and a sponge. Then I got out my supply of cotton waste and the can of Oxford brass polish. Savage *had 23 pieces of brass that I polished every sunny morning. Other responsibilities were sail drying, cleaning the cabin, and making sure the icebox was appropriately stocked for an afternoon's sail. Each morning I called Mr. Russell to find out the day's plan. If he were going sailing, I would plan for the usual 2 o'clock arrival of the launch and boarding party. The cockpit cushions had to be put out, the sail cover taken off, and everything made ready for almost instant departure. I took down the "owner absent" pennant just as the launch approached, belaying the halyard an instant before I had to reach out and help everyone climb on board.*

Dave left his mark. Writing to *Savage*'s current owner, who sails her in Turkey, he advised, "If you lie on the port forward bunk and look up at the deck stringers, you might see in faint pencil on one of them: 'THIS IS DAVID BURNHAM'S FAVORITE PLACE.' It's probably been painted over, but take a look for me."

The War Comes

The Rhodes 27s and Quincy Adams 17s had only two summers of sailing before war canceled sailing for three years. Everybody saw it coming. Already a base for the Coast Artillery at Fort Wright, Fishers was suddenly surrounded by military activity as New London's naval base and contractors began crash development programs. "The summer of 1940 saw a lot of war preparations," Herb Grandage reminisces, "and one could see and hear the PT boats going out for testing and for the most part being towed back into New London. During a couple of the sailboat races we had a close call or two with submarines which were also being tested out of New London. The soldiers at the fort were drilling. At night they would try to intercept planes overhead with a searchlight." When war came, a submarine net was laid across the mouth of the Thames River and opened when the Island ferry went and came. Recreational boating was restricted to coves and the small area south of the Hammocks and Dumplings.

Although most of the club's boats and many summer houses were mothballed, the yacht club opened for the summers. There was not much sailing and, in fact, little other activity except regular arguments between soldiers and the small staff as to why the Stars and Stripes flew lower on the yardarm than the club burgee. Dockmaster Jack Whiticar's explanations that this was normal flag etiquette, not an insult to the flag, changed no minds. Once victory was declared in Europe and wartime restrictions were eased, some boats went back into the water and the club slowly returned to normal in the summer of 1945. Soldiers were reassigned and disappeared completely a year later when Fort Wright was decommissioned.

Yet memories of wartime discomforts and adventures remained fresh. One year there was an unusually large run of mackerel in West Harbor. Due to gasoline rationing, none of the local fishermen could take advantage of this feast, but at least one current Fishers sailor, then a youngster, has a vivid memory of rowing out into the harbor and catching dozens of fish on handlines.

The wartime isolation ended in time for Fishers to welcome a foreign visitor without suspicion. A Swiss singlehanded sailor, Hans de Meiss-Teuffen, discovered this in July 1946 at the end of an east-to-west Atlantic crossing so rough and long that he wrote in his log, "Wonder if anybody else is ever so unlucky re wind and weather as I am!" After 58 days of this, Meiss-Teuffen made his landfall at Montauk Point and, late that night, finally came to rest without any idea where he was. "Am anchored off some shore, don't know which, shall find out at daybreak. There is a big place on shore with lots of lights. Hotel?" It was not a hotel. He was off the Fishers Island Club. Paddling ashore the next morning, he walked across the golf course and, reportedly with the assistance of a Swiss nanny, made friends who asked him to lunch. Unfortunately, before he could taste the Island's hospitality, *Speranza*'s anchor dragged, and she was drifting out on the ebb tide when the Coast Guard snagged and towed her into New London.

This picture postcard taken in the late 1940s shows the modest clubhouse and Jack Whiticar's colorful automobile. Tied up to the pier is one of the many big, high-speed commuter powerboats with which the yacht club became synonymous.

Courtesy Sara Porter

A Difficult Postwar Revival

Peacetime brought a mixed scene. Although the Island's summer population was growing, as was the club's fleet of elegant powerboats, the club's finances were limping along in an unsteady postwar economy that made it impossible to raise dues above nominal rates. After some talk of moving elsewhere, Commodores William Hubbard and John Nicholas Brown, with their board of governors, decided to make the club more attractive to new members. The first step was to create a larger facility on the site, which (with the clubhouse and the marina) was leased from Fishers Island Farms. Thanks to the recent closing of the Island's hotels, several small buildings were available. The club decided on the former quarters of the chef at the old Mansion House, which it bought for $800 and moved near the clubhouse for use as a storage facility and icehouse (it is now the site for offices, lockers, and showers). The club also extended its territory by leasing the property up to the fence around the neighboring gasoline station.

The club, meanwhile, whittled away at expenses until it finally succeeded in balancing the budget in 1949. Unfortunately, the membership simultaneously declined to less than 90. Next came an experiment in slashing dues and fees by 12 to 15 percent, but that did not attract enough new members to prevent a $2,500 shortfall. The officers then began to consider acquiring the property from Fishers Island Farms so the club would gain full control over the facility—including the full marina, with its slip rental fees.

134

(Above left) *The Browns showed off their fleet at Fishers Island in their 1947 Christmas card: The 38-foot powerboat* Hopak, *Nicholas Brown in the QA-17* Pavanne, *Carter Brown and his Bullseye* Conga, *Commodore and Anne Brown in the Wood Pussy* Polka, *and Angela Brown in her Weasel* Pirouette. Courtesy Sara Porter

(Above) *Commodore Brown (in shirt sleeves at the wheel) and his* Bolero *crew pose for the photographer before the start of the 1953 Newport-Annapolis Race.* 1984.187.136507F, © Mystic Seaport, Rosenfeld Collection

(Opposite) *John Nicholas Brown's magnificent 73-foot yawl* Bolero *struts along during the 1954 New York Yacht Club Cruise, five years after she was built to a Sparkman & Stephens design. Brown served as commodore of both the Fishers Island and the New York yacht clubs.* 1984.187.142496F, © Mystic Seaport, Rosenfeld Collection

The Brown Navy

Though a leader of one of Rhode Island's most storied families, John Nicholas Brown and his family spent most summers at Fishers while the three Brown children, Nick, Carter, and Angela, were growing up. The connection to the Island was through Anne Brown, whose father, Arthur B. Kinsolving, had been a summer rector at St. John's Church. Brown later was commodore of the New York Yacht Club, whose Newport clubhouse is his former home, Harbour Court.

The Brown family fleet was larger than most families. "In fact, we had quite a navy," recalls Nick Brown. The Christmas card for 1947 shows all the boats and their crews lined up. The family was for the moment between big boats. At the time this photograph was taken, Commodore Brown was planning his next boat with Olin Stephens, who was for mid and late twentieth-century yacht design what Herreshoff had been for his era. Brown said all he wanted was "a comfortable cruising boat with a turn of speed." What he got was a racy 73-foot yawl he named *Bolero*, which became the queen of the East Coast's ocean racing fleet and a class for the ages. Wherever *Bolero* cruised and raced, remembered Carter Brown, she "did cause something of a sensation in its ports of call, with flotillas of small boats coming to ogle this bellwether of the country's return to peacetime."

(Left) Among the many handsome family cruising boats that made their homes at Fishers after World War II was the Rhodes-designed sloop Windrift, *seen here with her proud owner, Joseph Middlebrook Jr., and his son Brad before she was launched at the Post yard on the Mystic River in 1947.* Mystic Seaport 1987.58.1451

(Bottom Left) The club launch, Active, *awaits its return to the water at the Post yard in Mystic.* Mystic Seaport 1987.58.1665

(Bottom Right) Ready for the season ahead at Hay Harbor, a Fishers Island Dumpling rests on blocks near Mrs. Fulton's June XVI *at the Post yard.* Mystic Seaport 1987.58.1443

From the Yard to the Race Course

There were many satisfactions to small-boat sailing. One of the top boats in 1950 was the Bullseye *Ghost*, under two 13-year-olds, Bill Ridgway and Mike Posey, who alternated at the helm, and occasionally with a third sailor. Half a century later, Posey looked back fondly on their relationship and its success: "Bill and I sailed together for so long that we never had to talk, because each knew what the other was thinking and produced the required result before it was requested. We managed to spook a lot of third-crew when they were needed, but it was great fun because execution was never a problem. We were free to think our way around the course without worrying about how to make the boat do what we wanted. All this at the age of 13. I profoundly wish I could still do it."

The club's Quincy Adams 17 Season Championship trophy was awarded from 1946 to 1952. Jean McIntire won it in 1946, Bradley Middlebrook in 1947-48, Nick Brown in 1949-51, and J.P. Osborn in 1952

(Right) *A Dumpling (right), a Skiddoo, and other junior boats diverge on a quiet afternoon in Hay Harbor.* Henry L. Ferguson Museum

(Bottom) *On a warm and windless August morning in 1948, Reynolds du Pont's commuter* Goddess *tows a flotilla of H-23s and QA-17s across Fishers Island Sound to participate in the Ram Island Race. Eliot Porter's* Red Cap *is at center.* Henry L. Ferguson Museum

1950 Season Champions

Bullseye Class, *Wednesday Season Series*
1st – *Bunker Hill*, Frank Polk
2nd – *Ghost*, Mike Posey

Bullseye Class, *Saturday Season Series*
1st – *Ghost*, Bill Ridgway
2nd – *Bunker Hill*, Frank Polk

Quincy Adams Class, *Wednesday Season Series*
1st – *Pavanne*, Nick Brown
2nd – *Windrift*, Jr., Brad Middlebrook

Quincy Adams Class, *Saturday Season Series*
1st – *Windrift, Jr.*, Brad Middlebrook
2nd – *Sea Gull*, John Wilmerding

Handicap Class Saturday Season Series
1st – *Kandi Chips*, Reynolds du Pont

The New Commuters

The small marina was becoming the club's centerpiece because the fleet was changing dramatically. The schooner had once been the glamour boat. Now it was the commuter powerboat.

Already a center for handsome powerboats, the Fishers Island Yacht Club after the war became one of the East Coast's centers of the high-speed, powerful boats that were known as commuters because their owners often used then to get to work. The fleet included Laurence Rockefeller's *Dauntless*, with twin PT-type engines; Reynolds du Pont's *Goddess*; Everett Dickinson's Trumpy *Alva*, in which he commuted between Fishers and Essex; and the various *Blue Hens*, including a magnificent 72-foot Trumpy, owned by the Riegels. Roger Firestone had *Rock Bottom*, one of the smallest at 42 feet but with plenty of muscle to compensate, and later the triple-engine *Tireless* (an appropriate name for a boat owned by a tire manufacturer). "When either *Rock Bottom* or *Tireless* started up," recalls Chris Roosevelt, "you could hear the engines miles away. And when they revved up to racing speeds, you definitely got out of the way." When young Chip du Pont heard *Rock Bottom* start up, he would ask his mother to take him down to the water so he could watch her accelerate down Fishers Island Sound.

The best known of them was the famous 45-knot *Aphrodite III*, owned by John Hay "Jock" Whitney Jr., a prominent New York investor and newspaper publisher (unrelated to Commodore Arthur Whitney). If this voluptuous, glossy black, 74-foot pow-

The new breed of commuters that filled the club's slips after the war were high powered and exciting to watch. (Above) *Jock Whitney's 45-knot black bullet,* Aphrodite, *was almost 10 years old when she began coming to Fishers Island in 1947. Here, she shows Whitney's allegiance to Yale as she blasts up the Thames River for a Harvard-Yale Race.* 1984.187.96873F © Mystic Seaport, Rosenfeld Collection

(Upper right) *Roger Firestone's* Rock Bottom, *a 42-foot C. Raymond Hunt design, appeared at Fishers in 1950.* Morris Rosenfeld photo. 1984.187.129970F © Mystic Seaport, Rosenfeld Collection

(Lower right) *With her twin V-12s, one of the most dramatic commuters was Laurence Rockefeller's 65-foot aluminum-hulled* Dauntless, *designed by Sparkman & Stephens in 1947.* Morris Rosenfeld photo. 1984.187.147493F © Mystic Seaport, Rosenfeld Collection

One of the most active commuters was Reynolds du Pont's Goddess, *a 58-foot Consolidated commuter launched in 1947. She could travel at speed but often served as tender to the racing fleet.* Morris Rosenfeld photo. 1984.187.133037F © Mystic Seaport, Rosenfeld Collection

(Right) *Roger Firestone's 67-foot Trumpy cruiser,* Tireless, *driven by twin 12-cylinder diesels, joined the Fishers fleet in 1963.* Stanley Rosenfeld photo. ANN.1984.187.5679, © Mystic Seaport, Rosenfeld Collection

erhouse stimulated plenty of envy, it was poetic justice because she was a product of envy. When his previous *Aphrodite* sucked exhaust one too many times from his brother-in-law Charles Shipman Payson's commuter, Whitney went to the Purdy Boat Co. for a new boat. She spent the war in the Coast Guard, running up and down the Hudson to President Roosevelt's home at Hyde Park, and by the time she started coming to Fishers, in 1947, *Aphrodite* was on her third set of engines—twin 1,500-horsepower V-12 Packards that made a boom audible across Fishers Island Sound, belching so much smoke that one of Charlie and Alice Ferguson's daughters nicknamed her "dirty diapers." According to another powerboatman, who made the mistake of trying to outpace *Aphrodite*, "Jock opened his thing up when I tried to pass him and nearly washed me onto the shore." When youngsters out for a sail heard *Aphrodite* coming—say, on a run to New London to pick up the morning *New York Herald-Tribune*—they would race over and try to surf her enormous wake. According to his biographer, E.J. Kahn Jr., when someone asked Whitney why he had bought the newspaper, Whitney replied with a laugh that "some rich men had yachts, some had mistresses, and some had newspapers." Commented Kahn, "He was rich enough, of course, to have all three."

Hurricane Carol in 1954 left many piles of wreckage, including this boat on the club pier. Courtesy Sara Porter

The Year of the Hurricanes

The worst decade for weather in Fishers Island's recent history was the 1950s, when 11 tropical storms came within 180 miles of New London. Since many of them passed to the west, Fishers was frequently caught in the dangerous sector of the storm's right shoulder, where the wind blows hardest. In 1954 alone, hurricanes Carol and Edna hit the Island just 11 days apart (a third hurricane that year, Hazel, drowned Pennsylvania and upstate New York). When Carol heaved an 85-knot wind and a 10-foot storm surge at Fishers, Charlie Ferguson was persuaded to hoist his house, Flounder In, another 18 inches higher in order, he explained, "to let the next extreme tide pass under it instead of through it."

Beaches spat up any number of objects, including old ship hulls and piles of pig iron ballast. Reyn du Pont's Grey Gulls, the site of the old Sage Brick Works, was showered in bricks. "That house was covered in bricks," recalls his son Chip. "We spent two days with wheelbarrows trying to dump those bricks where the seawall used to be." Though the yacht club's docks and launches were beaten up, the fleet was not badly damaged because Jack Whiticar, the manager, and his staff, and the boat captains (to quote Reyn du Pont) performed "acts that bordered on heroism." In thanks, the club awarded bonus checks to the staff and Zippo wind-proof cigarette lighters to the boat captains.

As the new commuters appeared in the late 1940s, Aphrodite *(the second larger boat out from the shore) was assigned slip No. 1 in the club's small marina.* Courtesy Sara Porter

A Declaration of Independence

The many commuters presented the club with a problem and an opportunity. When Jock Whitney first came to the Island in 1947, he instructed his captain to dock *Aphrodite III* in an open slip. Unaware that the space had been assigned to someone else by Fishers Island Farms, Whitney was taken aback by a scolding letter from Pete du Pont, then the club's secretary-treasurer, who insisted, "You were docking your boat on someone else's money." Whitney paid the bill (for $240) but told du Pont that he did not understand why such an explosion had arisen from his inadvertent error. In time, Whitney was forgiven and *Aphrodite* was assigned slip No. 1, the place of honor.

The core problem for the club remained: it did not control its facility. So long as the slips were controlled by Fishers Island Farms, the club did not have ultimate authority over slip assignments and maintenance and had no income from the marina other than commissions. With many proud owners hungry for so few slips, and with complaints mounting that the Farms was stinting on repairs, the officers proposed to take over the club's buildings and marina. The members needed convincing. "Considerable discussion was held on this move," say the minutes of the 1952 general meeting—code words indi-

As the marina grew, its slips housed regulars like Rock Bottom *(center) and visitors like* Foto *(far left), the chase boat for the Rosenfeld family of photographers, here making a stop during the 1957 New York Yacht Club Cruise.* Morris Rosenfeld photo. 1984.187.156491F © Mystic Seaport, Rosenfeld Collection

cating that the debate was heated before the club bought the marina and clubhouse for $5,100. Although several thousand dollars was donated to the club that year, a bank loan was needed to spruce up the marina. As soon as those repairs were completed, Hurricane Carol tore the piers up and the club had to borrow more money to patch them up. Within a few years the club was saddled with a debt of $15,000—the equivalent of almost $100,000 today—that even the efforts and the charity of the "good fairies" could not dent. Despite trimming overhead, raising fees, and aggressively recruiting members, the club staggered along. "It was again noted that the Club operated at a loss for the year," read the minutes of a board of governors' meeting in 1956.

The reality was clear and the club surrendered to it. "You just couldn't make ends meet here," recalls Harris Parsons. In 1962 the yacht club sold the marina, land, and clubhouse to the Fishers Island Development Company (FIDCO), the successor to the company that had developed the Island's east end. The next year Reyn du Pont finally reported a profit, cautiously.

Captain Pete

The postwar period was a time of powerful boats, powerful captains, and powerful commodores. Some have called it the era of the du Ponts.

Pete du Pont first served as a yacht club officer in 1936, and almost a quarter century later he completed a nine-year term as commodore (the longest in the club's history), only to serve as his brother Reyn's vice commodore. (Later du Pont commodores were Reyn's son Chip and his cousins Jerry and Sandy Riegel.) The du Ponts first came to Fishers in the early 1920s, and by 1938 the family fleet at Fishers consisted of eight boats, including Pete's schooner *Barlovento*, the L-16s *Starboard* and *Port*, the H-23s *Crenthozy* and *Nitromon* (named for an explosive manufactured by the family firm), and some powerboats. Pete's wife, Jane, would later acquire one of the more unusual vessels in the club's fleet, a Royal Navy captain's pinnace, *Maid of Honor*.

Barlovento (Spanish for "windward") was built in 1932, and Pete immediately took her to sea as the first Fishers Island boat to sail a Newport-Bermuda Race. (This race is closely identified with the family; du Pont is the second most popular name of skippers in its long history after "Smith.") She was fourth to finish in her maiden race, and later won many races off Fishers in her nearly 30 years under du Pont's command. At last report, the schooner *Barlovento* was still sailing in the Pacific Northwest.

Her successor was a Philip Rhodes-designed steel 72-foot centerboard ketch, *Barlovento II*. She came to life in a hard blow. In her first Bermuda Race, in 1960, she carried a full mainsail through a gale. Bill Robinson of *Yachting* magazine was in her crew and described the experience this way: "Smashing ahead in the rain that stings like shotgun pellets, throwing spray over her whole length as she rears and plunges over the steep, tumbling waves, *Barlovento* drives on for Bermuda." A year later she won a Memorial Day Block Island Race in a snowstorm. Almost half the fleet dropped out, but *Barlovento II*, again not reefing, was first to finish and won

"The skipper maintains a stoical calm," Bill Robinson wrote of Pete du Pont in a storm at sea. Here Captain Pete enjoys a moment of bliss on board Barlovento *in 1948. Two generations of Fishers sailors crewed for him.*

Courtesy Sara Porter

on corrected time. Ironically, her only gear failure was the heating system that would have made her crew even more comfortable.

"The skipper maintains a stoical calm, and no one says much," Robinson reported about du Pont during the 1960 Bermuda Race gale. The 1972 Newport-Bermuda Race saw even worse conditions, and the big ketch took on enough green water to trigger the inflation mechanism on her life raft, and she finished with it partly deflated. For a few hours in that race, du Pont stood by a disabled boat until a Coast Guard vessel arrived.

In 1980, one of *Barlovento II*'s regular crew, Charles Brainard, rented a house on Fishers for two weeks. One day he ran into du Pont. "Captain Pete was his normal wonderful self," Brainard remembers. "He growled at me, 'Did you get caught in the kelp net?' Then he told me to look in my mailbox in a couple of days. There I found a guest card for the Big Club." Brainard later received another letter informing him, to his complete surprise, that he had been accepted into the golf club's membership. In time he learned Pete du Pont had choreographed every step. After such a welcome, Brainard decided that, since he was a club member, he might as well buy a house on the Island.

(Above) The crew for the 1960 Bermuda Race poses on board the ketch Barlovento II. *Captain Pete is at the wheel, Captain Nils Jackson and the paid hands are at left, John Wilmerding stands at the rail at center, and the boating author Bill Robinson is second from right in the back row.* Morris Rosenfeld photo. 1984.187.166217F, © Mystic Seaport, Rosenfeld Collection

(Left) Maid of Honor, *Jane du Pont's 55-foot British Admiralty pinnace, built in 1927, turned heads wherever she went.* Mystic Seaport 1968-9-38H

Barlovento II

The second *Barlovento* was a 72-foot Rhodes-designed steel ketch that took unique pleasure in strong winds. With a shallow draft for island cruising, she was equipped with two centerboards, which could be adjusted to counterbalance any combination of sails. Launched by Abeking & Rasmussen at Lemwerder, Germany, in 1959, she quickly earned a reputation as the most comfortable Bermuda racer and one of the most successful ocean racers of her time.

(Far left) Barlovento II *was large enough to accommodate a large center cockpit without looking distorted.* Morris Rosenfeld photo. 1984.187.163676F © Mystic Seaport, Rosenfeld Collection

(Above left) *The owner's stateroom had the nautical equivalent of Swedish modern decor.* Morris Rosenfeld photo. 1984.187.163687F © Mystic Seaport, Rosenfeld Collection

(Left) *Her interior was brighter and more open than the first* Barlovento*'s. Here are the crew's forecastle accommodations and head.* Morris Rosenfeld photo. (1984.187.163674F © Mystic Seaport, Rosenfeld Collection

(Above) Barlovento II*'s sail plan was smaller and more compact than the schooner's, and much easier to manage. She raced often and cruised widely.* 1984.187.163678F ©Mystic Seaport, Rosenfield Collection

The Banker: Reyn du Pont

A yacht club's day-to-day operations are in the hands of a couple of dedicated volunteers and a few employees. At Fishers, a hierarchy ran down from the officers to the manager, and then through the professional captains to the college kids who drove the launches, raised the flags, and polished the brass.

"The Fishers Island Yacht Club is a very informal affair," Reynolds du Pont once told a prospective member, explaining why it had taken so long for him to process some paperwork. As secretary-treasurer from 1948 until 1959 (when he jumped from the fire into the frying pan and became commodore), Reyn du Pont was, as he put it, "the seagoing banker of the outfit." He wrote the checks, recruited new members, struggled to unite sailors and powerboaters, handled the sometimes tricky negotiations with club manager Jack Whiticar, and juggled dock space among captains of Wall Street and industry. He obviously enjoyed it because once his term as commodore was over, du Pont put in another three years as secretary-treasurer.

Reyn du Pont's mantra was that anybody who used the club should join the club. He was mystified that this rule was not obvious to everybody else. Whenever the name of a likely candidate appeared, he sent out the necessary paperwork without going through the formality of finding a proposer. Usually the fellow joined up, but sometimes there were problems.

A summer person who requested a non-resident membership on the grounds that he docked his boat in Pirate's Cove received the following reply from the exasperated du Pont: "We do not have a non-resident membership for either 'Cove Dwellers' or even dwellers in the United States. However, our dues are only $30 a season for a senior membership plus $6 Federal Tax. As you are probably aware, the Club dispenses soft drinks, ice, and a limited supply of club burgees, etc., and we will be very happy to take care of your needs, if possible." Whether the fellow changed his mind is not known, but du Pont must have gained some satisfaction from venting his frustration.

All that time, he did his best to get out in one or another of his own boats, like the 1907 steam launch *Chester Belle* and his cruising boat *Alinda II*. One September, he wrote a member who had expressed a concern: "Thank you for your letter of August 5, 1954, and we are sorry that we are so tardy in answering it. August seems to have passed very rapidly and with the rash of over-abundant sailing breezes over the end of the month, things have been at sixes and eights in the Yacht Club." That was the price of getting in a little sailing.

Reynolds du Pont races his yawl Alinda *in Off Soundings with Geddes and Harris Parsons in the crew. The 33-foot* Alinda *was a K. Aage Nielsen design, built in 1955.* Courtesy Geddes Parsons

Jack Whiticar, the club's long-time manager, and his wife, Alice, enjoy a happy moment on board one of his powerboats in 1948. Courtesy Sara Porter

Jack Whiticar

"I figure I am getting paid as much for what I know as for what I do," Jack Whiticar, the club's longtime manager once wrote Pete du Pont. "I started working for the club in 1933, and in all those years we have never had anybody lose his life or get seriously injured. I'd hate to count all the times I have kept people from doing damn fool things, and got them out of it when they did." Nicknamed "Woodpecker" for a piercing voice that could be heard across the harbor, Whiticar was a gifted mechanic, a brilliant seaman, and a powerful presence. Harris Parsons recalls happily, "Jack was a fixture at the yacht club. He would do anything."

For almost 40 years John Hogate Whiticar Jr. and his wife, Alice, split time between Fishers and Stuart, Florida, as he ran the docks, managed the club, or, at the end of his career, served as captain aboard Jock Whitney's last *Aphrodite*. For many years his brothers, Buster and Johnson, also worked at West Harbor. Sons of the professional captain for Irving Bonbright, the Whiticars had roots deep in the Island and in Stuart, where they ran a charter fishing boat, *The Three Brothers*, and built boats, including the last *Aphrodite*. Come spring, Jack engaged in a long, playful negotiation with his friend Reyn du Pont concerning housing and pay, eventually made a deal, and drove back north for another season of managing things at West Harbor.

The Captains

(Left) Walter Bohlen was in charge of Franklin Haines's schooners named Marita. *Father of club member Frank Bohlen, he is seen here in 1936.* Courtesy W. Frank Bolen

(Right) Johan Johansen was captain or mate on yachts for many years and lived to the age of 106. Fishers Island Gazette

When Fishers was a haven for large yachts, the piers and club grounds were populated by professional sailors who were easily identified by their khaki uniforms, dark tans, rolling gaits, hand-rolled cigarettes, unsubtle opinions, and unfamiliar accents—Norwegian from Olaf (Ollie) Jensen, or the South Florida twang of Jack Whiticar. The captain's job was to manage the boat when the owner was not aboard. Many also were in charge when the owner was aboard, although their authority was displayed with greater subtlety than when the blue "owner absent" pennant flew in the starboard rigging. Some captains also served as sailing instructors for the owner's family. Nick Brown, for example, learned most of his sailing from the captains of his father's big yachts, Captain Alfred Weebe from *Saraband* and Fred Lawton, the skipper of *Bolero*.

These were strong men, and strong-minded, too. When Nils Jackson, the ketch *Barlovento II*'s professional captain, saw an amateur sailor lounging in the Dyer Dhow dinghy under the mizzen boom, he growled, "Get outta my dinghy boat!" Their political opinions could and did shock the nice, liberally educated boys and girls of the Fishers Island Yacht Club. More than one professional captain carried a gun in his car, even at Fishers. Holly

The professional captains were important and highly visible members of the Fishers Island Yacht Club community into the 1970s. Here, a group of captains in their khaki uniforms discuss the day's activities on the club pier around 1960. Henry L. Ferguson Museum

Hollenbeck, who managed the club after Jack Whiticar retired, contemptuously referred to sailboats as "blow boats." Once a year the sailors got their revenge on the stink-potters in the professional skippers' race, sailed singlehanded in Bullseyes for the Bent Propeller Trophy. The pros were always badly beaten by the college kids serving as paid hands on smaller boats.

Though they could seem intimidating, most captains were as gentle as lambs and often invited the boys to dinner aboard the luxury yachts when the owners were absent. Many pros and their wives became members of the Island's family. Frank Bohlen's father, Walter, from Germany, was captain of Franklin Haines's Alden schooners *Marita*, and Herb Ahlgren's father was steward on board Mortimer Buckner's big yawl *Pampero* under one of the Island's most respected captains, George "Gus" Olsen.

Captain Johan Johansen spent a third of his long life on or near Fishers. Raised on a family farm in Norway, he went to sea at the age of 14 and at 17 immigrated to the United States in 1909. He joined the Revenue Cutter Service (a predecessor to the U.S. Coast Guard) and eventually came to Fishers in 1934 to work under Captain Olsen in Mortimer Buckner's yachts. Later he worked for Walter S. Carpenter Jr., first aboard the 66-foot Consolidated commuter yacht *Grey Gull* and later as captain of *Grey Gull II* and caretaker of the Grey Gulls estate. Captain Johansen raised children and grandchildren on the Island, was a member of the Fishers Island Fire Department, and commanded the local American Legion post. He finally left Fishers in 1972 at the age of 80. "He loved the Island," said his son John at his father's hundredth birthday. "He'd still be there now, but my mother insisted that he leave. She knew he would never retire unless he left." Johansen died in Florida in 1991 at the age of 106.

The loss of his right arm did not stop Ed Hedge when it came to lobstering or other activities on the water.

New London Day photo, Courtesy Hedge family

Ed Hedge

Among the more remarkable characters in the Island's maritime history was Edmund Hedge. A member of a Fishers family that arrived in the 1870s, he was a lobsterman, ran a village fish market, and succeeded Skip Lawson as the man who tended moorings and towed small boats from and to their off-season berths. Remarkably, Ed Hedge accomplished this with only one arm, having lost the other as a boy when a shotgun accidentally discharged. His ability to organize a long tow of boats or set a mooring literally single-handed was legendary.

Around West Harbor, Ed Hedge was the boss. "In those years there was no paperwork," recalls Gus Kinsolving, a lifelong Fishers cruising sailor. "Moorings went where Ed Hedge put them." After Eliot Porter bought his new cruising sloop *Chrisada* in 1966, his father, Maxwell, negotiated with Hedge about the boat's mooring and the family Bullseye. Bertha Hedge replied for her husband in a letter so informative and delightful in its directness that it should be quoted in full:

Ed. will bring over your Bullseye. About the new boat. Ed wishes to know if you think a 400 lb. mushroom would be the size for the large boat. Do you wish Nylon line? Ed says that will last for three or four years. You will need about 30 feet of chain, shackles etc. Also when will you want this done—

Sincerely,

Bertha S. Hedge—(Mrs. Ed)

The Porters said they preferred a nylon rode over natural fibers, and wanted *Chrisada* moored near where the schooner *Barlovento* used to lie. Ed Hedge's bill totaled $279.77, including $5 for splicing the nylon line.

Captains and launch boys shown include (back row) Doug Baldwin (Seyon), Holly Hollenbeck (dockmaster), Pete Sinclair Sr. (Goddess) and (front row) Dick Hale (launch driver) and Jack Whiticar (Aphrodite). Courtesy Sara Porter

The Launch Boys

While the club's style was informal, flag etiquette was taken with utmost seriousness and enforced sternly by Jack Whiticar and the yacht owners. This meant that one of the most important duties for a launch boy and paid hand was making Colors, meaning to fire the club's cannon ashore and hoist the American flag precisely at 0800 in the morning, and fire another cannon and lower the flag at exact sunset. As Dave Burnham remembers, "We followed the rigid protocol of Colors in those days, priding ourselves at being on board at 0759 to put the colors up at the 0800 firing of the yacht club's cannon. We were even more careful to take the flag down when the sunset gun was fired."

At the bottom of the yacht club organization chart, but always observant, were the college kids who ran the launches. One was Herb Grandage:

The launch, Active, *was basically the responsibility of the launch boy who ran in and out of the harbor all day. Johnson Whiticar's job was to pretty much see that the boats at the dock were taken care of, and Jack, who was the boss, handled the phone, the members, and, in general, the policy of the club. The exception for running the launch was the moment the commodore arrived and immediately Jack was the launch driver and the everyday launch boy was sent to clean the john, mow the lawn, dab a little paint here or there.*

On occasion fog would shut in so heavy one could not see ten feet. The ferryboat was very late and docked adjacent to the yacht club. On those occasions Jack would take the launch, compass in hand, and proceed to the end of the Island and lead the ferry into the dock. The launch boy was directed to sit in the stern and advise Jack if he was proceeding in a straight line. It worked well.

Deckhand Keith Ahlgren, Captain Gus Olsen, and Steward Al Ahlgren smile for the camera on board Mrs. W. Shirley Fulton's power yacht June XVI *in 1965.* Courtesy Keith Ahlgren

A Deckhand's Duties

One of the club's most senior captains, Olsen (and Al Ahlgren too) had been aboard Mortimer N. Buckner's yachts until the 1938 hurricane sank Buckner's *Pampero* and *Ruth*. The Olsen family spent their winters in Brooklyn until 1940, when Olsen, who until then had worked mostly in racing sailboats, took over command of a powerboat in Florida. He later returned to Fishers. Keith Alghren, Al's son, reminisced about his own duties other than handling docking lines:

I worked on the June XVI *as a deckhand/steward for three summers. The* June*'s cruises were usually day trips to the Connecticut shoreline, up the river to Mystic Seaport, around the Island, and especially Watch Hill, Rhode Island, the favorite lunch stop for Mrs. Fulton. Besides cleaning and polishing the woodwork and brass, my role was to serve sandwiches, cakes/cookies, soft drinks (grape juice), and tea/coffee (no liquor) to the guests in the stern sitting area (40 pillows on the couch).*

Commodore Harris Parsons happily rigs the family Bullseye in 1963. Courtesy Sara Porter

1961 Season Champions

Bullseye Class
Wednesday Season Series
1st – Harry Ferguson
2nd – Kandi du Pont

Bullseye Class
Saturday Season Series
1st – Talcott Stanley
2nd – Harry Ferguson

Quincy Adams Class
Wednesday Season Series
1st – Missy Ridgway
2nd – Mrs. Henry C. Osborne

Quincy Adams Class
Saturday Season Series
1st – Mrs. Henry C. Osborne
2nd – P.S. du Pont IV/ Dedo du Pont

Off Soundings and the Parsons Trophy

The yacht club, of course, was not just about Colors, commodores, and captains. In the 1950s and '60s, sailors began to get away from the Island a little more often to sail in events sponsored by other clubs. The most popular in local waters were the Off Soundings Club's spring and fall race weekends and the Parsons Trophy team races.

A number of cruising boat sailors were active in the Off Soundings Club. Founded in 1933 in Springfield, Massachusetts, by three landlocked salt-water sailors, after the war it became one of New England's largest big-boat sailing associations, with more than 600 members and 450 boats in its 50th anniversary year of 1983, and with a full racing schedule in the waters between New London, Block Island, and Shelter Island. The club is a sailing club; no powerboat owner should even think of applying for membership. Eager for the largest possible turnout, it has always imposed rules intended to give everybody a good chance of winning any race. For many years the club had its own extremely simple handicap rule, and it continues to handicap successful skippers. Fishers Island Yacht Club has had two Off Soundings commodores, Eliot Porter and Frank Bohlen.

The other major interclub institution is the Parsons Trophy series. First sailed in 1953, it celebrates a friendship among neighbors from Short Hills, New Jersey, who summered on one shore or another of Fishers Island Sound. Joseph L. and Mary Louise Parsons came to Fishers, while Robert and Libby Johnstone summered at Stonington (Libby Johnstone's parents had in fact become engaged on Fishers in 1903). After Mary Louise Parsons died of cancer in 1953, the Johnstones presented a trophy in her memory for a team race rotating annually among three local sailing clubs: Wadawanuck at Stonington, Watch Hill, and Fishers Island. Relations among the three clubs had long been close, with several families holding joint memberships. They shared the same approach. As the

Johnstones' son Rodney (the designer of the J/Boat line) says, "These clubs up here are real yacht clubs—no bar, no restaurant. The whole idea is for people to get together for friendly competition. Protests are discouraged, and there's a pretty high level of sportsmanship."

After the golden anniversary Parsons Trophy regatta in 2003, won by the Fishers team, there had been 48 team races (the others were canceled due to weather). The record was Wadawanuck, 19 wins; Fishers Island, 16 wins; and Watch Hill, 13 wins.

The spring and fall Off Soundings Club races have long attracted serious Fishers Island Yacht Club racers. Geordie Loveday and Sara Porter's Jolly Mon *rounds a mark in tight quarters during a 2003 race.* Bill Pepin photo. Courtesy Bill Pepin

At the 1977 Bullseye Nationals, the first such championship hosted at the Fishers Island Yacht Club, Commodore David Harris (in dark cap at right center) talks with visiting sailors during a reception on the club lawn. John Harper photo. Courtesy David Burnham

"The Energy Within the Club"
New Generations Sail into a New Century, 1970-2003

Life changed in West Harbor. Even as *A Cruising Guide to the New England Coast* was praising the club for its "many fine yachts," the big commuters slipped away and West Harbor was abuzz with small powerboats. In 1970 there were 335 members paying low annual dues of $20 for individuals and $30 for an entire family. Almost half the club's fleet of 104 boats consisted of powerboats. There were 29 auxiliary sailboats and only 25 pure sailboats, all but a handful from the one remaining keelboat racing class, the Bullseye, after the remaining Quincy Adams 17s burned up in a fire at Mystic Shipyard. Once, the major concern had been finding enough racing boats for sailors, young and old. Now people were focusing their energies on opposing a scheme to build a bridge across eastern Long Island Sound to Watch Hill, using Fishers Island as one support.

A few things remained constant, like the many anonymous "good fairies" who donated money, time, and services to the yacht club. Their spirit was exemplified by the commodores who succeeded the du Ponts in the period 1962-75: Harris B. Parsons, Talcott Stanley, David H. Harris, Michael Laughlin, Eliot H. Porter II, and Burton J. Tremaine Jr. With a system of two-year terms, plus a policy of electing active sailors, these and later officers stayed in close touch with the club's activities. "If a boat got in trouble, David Harris was there to tow us in," recalls Sara Porter. "When Allie Evans and I were dismasted as we jibed around Dumpling Bell, there he was." Parents brought food down to the club, helped with programs, and kept a close watch—the more anxious of them keeping a lookout on the race course from "Nervous Mothers' Point," near the Three Sisters.

And there remained a profound sense of place. Children and grandchildren of club founders were everywhere, recreating their youthful summers. "The only time I wasn't here was my four years in the Navy," Sandy Riegel says. "I kept coming here. I stayed here."

As comfortable as it seemed, the Fishers Island Yacht Club was undergoing a transition that, though not always clear, led in time to the present-day club. Although Commodore Porter was a third-generation Fishers summer person, he was sure the club needed to enlarge its mission. In his retirement speech in 1973, Porter made three points. First, sailors in the last one-design class, the Bullseyes, should get out more and travel off-Island to the national championship. Second, the club needed a well-organized junior sailing program in coordination with the Hay Harbor Club. And third, it was time to establish another "new strong racing fleet."

Eliot Porter

Eliot Porter began his sailing career in the Bullseye Viking *and raced and cruised for many years in the H-23* Red Cap *(ex-*Padick*).*

Courtesy Sara Porter

One of the Island's best-known sailors was Eliot Porter. Thanks to his mastery of the tricky local conditions, hard-earned in a lifetime of weekend racing against clever opponents like Talcott Stanley, he was among the most successful sailors on Fishers Island Sound. "These guys knew these waters," Chip du Pont says of Porter and Stanley. "They knew where to be there, and when to be there. You had a 4-knot head tide, and these guys could go by like they were on railroad tracks."

After losing his Bullseye in the 1938 hurricane and then serving in World War II, Porter bought Everett Dickinson's Herreshoff 23 *Padick*. Renaming her *Red Cap*, he sailed whenever and wherever he could, including with his wife Marilyn on their honeymoon. Bruce May has said that one of his fondest memories was "seeing Eliot Porter sailing down harbor solo in *Red Cap*, en route to Block Island." In 1966 Porter bought a Hinckley Pilot 35 sloop that he named *Chrisada* (a combination of the names of his children, Christopher, Sara, and David) and in which he raced and cruised for almost thirty years, for much of that time against Stanley in his own Pilot, *Bagheera*. ("I rarely beat *Chrisada*," Stanley admitted.)

The world of *Chrisada* was a complete one, with cruises to Maine, many races, regular social gatherings, funny crew newsletters, and lots of music played by pick-up orchestras and sung using an eclectic song book that Porter assembled. His friends were many. A few months after Porter's death in 2002, on the day of his birthday, Charlie Ferguson took the sizeable risk of port-tacking the fleet at the Bullseye National Championship, sailed on the Sound. Ferguson, who won the race, later explained that he wanted to do something dramatic in memory of his dear friend Eliot Porter.

(Left) Whether boiling along under spinnaker off Block Island during an Off Soundings race or cruising more sedately with family, the Hinckley Pilot Chrisada *served well for nearly 30 years.* Photo by Ted Kelley, Photo-Boat

(Below) Courtesy Sara Porter

(Above right) In 1987, Bill and Eileen Ames, Eliot Porter, and Jean and Bruce May represented the club in the South Pacific aboard the Sea Cloud. *Back in West Harbor, Porter might be found showing the club colors in a handsome St. Lawrence River skiff.* Courtesy Sara Porter

John, Steve, and Dave Burnham show off their first-place trophy at the Bullseye Nationals in Marblehead, Massachusetts, in 1976. At right are Peter Vincent and Ginny Rinkle of Rockport, Massachusetts.

John Harper photo. Courtesy Dave Burnham

Bullseye Travels

The first of Porter's concerns lay with the Bullseyes. In what Harris Parsons calls "the era of the Whaler," only the Bullseye was left for older juniors and adults. One of the first classes to shift to fiberglass construction soon after World War II, the boat was also improved by the addition of cuddies, spinnakers, and larger jibs. By the 1960s, only one wooden Bullseye was still racing at Fishers, her red topsides so discolored that she was nicknamed "the stewed prune."

While there were plenty of Bullseyes sailing, not all were racing, and none ventured off-Island except on the occasional junior cruise or team race, or to latch onto Ed Hedge's towline to the shipyard in September. The Fishers Bullseye fleet was so introverted that in 1969 a Bullseye Class officer, like a colonial secretary inquiring about a remote outpost, wrote the club to ask if any Bullseye racing was going on at the Island.

When a Fishers boat finally ventured to a Bullseye National Championship in 1975, it began an uninterrupted string not only of participation but of strong performances. That first crew was a family team that included two future club commodores. John Burnham was at the tiller while his father Dave and brother Steve trimmed sails. They won the national championship that year and also in 1976. In 1977, the nationals were held at Fishers—the first major sailing championship held at the Island—and Steve Burnham won, with Eliot Porter in second place. Later, Dave Burnham would win four nationals as skipper, sometimes after sailing his boat to the regatta, even navigating the Cape Cod Canal. ("There's sort of a habit in this family for trying to set distance records," says Steve Burnham, who, like his father, has rowed around Fishers Island. Steve once was attempting to circumnavigate Fishers in a Sunfish when the rudder broke and he was blown to Montauk.)

In all, Fishers Island Yacht Club sailors won 12 of the 29 Bullseye National Championships between 1975 and 2003. Dave, Steve, and John Burnham between them won seven, while Peter or Caroline Rugg won a total of five. In all those years, a Fishers boat finished lower than fifth place only four times. (See Appendix 2 for a summary of Fishers results at Bullseye Championships.)

(Top) *Dave Burnham's* Querida, *#80, gains an edge at the start of a race at Marion, Massachusetts, during the 2003 Bullseye Nationals, a series won by the 48-year-old boat with Steve and Paul Burnham crewing.* © Anne Converse

(Above) *The club was well represented at the 2000 Bullseye Nationals at Card Sound, Key Largo, Florida with (from left) Bruce Beggs, Basil Vasilou, Paul Burnham and son David, Dave Burnham, Brad Burnham Jr., Peter Rugg, and Cal Beggs (kneeling). The team of Rugg and Vasilou came in second overall.* Lucy Otzen photo

"Bullseyes at Dumpling Bell," painted by Charlie Ferguson, is awarded to the top Fishers Island boat at the Bullseye National Championship. The artist himself had several high finishes at the nationals.

1974 Series Standings and Trophies

Bullseye Class
Wednesday Season Series
- 1st – Steve Burnham, *Sea Witch*
- 2nd – Geb Cook (assisted by Bobby Campbell), *Sandpiper*
- 3rd – Ashley and Laurie Riegel (with Allegra Braga and Diane Furse), *Neptune*

Bullseye Class
Saturday Season Series
- 1st – Charles Ferguson, *Pegasus*
- 2nd – Harris Parsons, *Sandpiper*
- 3rd – Stowe Phelps, *Little Goodie*

Harris Trophy
'Round Island Race
- Burton G. Tremaine Jr., *Kachina*

Burt Tremaine's Kachina *gets set to trail to the 1978 Half Ton North Americans in Annapolis, Maryland.* John Burnham photo

Burton Tremaine

Burton Tremaine was such a cagey racing skipper that he kept a pipe on board solely to make smoke to trace the zephyrs in a calm. After racing Bullseyes for many years, Tremaine in 1973 acquired the first of three ocean racers he named *Kachina*, each about 35 feet long. He did well in Off Soundings events and traveled to major championships (he finished second in a New York Yacht Club 36 nationals). In his crews were many of the next generation of Fishers sailors, including his son Tony, John and Kathy Harris, Brad Burnham III, Chris Thatcher, Bill McCance, and John Burnham, who got his start in boating journalism through his travels with Burt Tremaine. Other than doing well, Tremaine was well known for caring for his boat and always having the best gear. "Every time he stepped on his boat it was immaculate," Tony has said.

'Round Island Race

As far as Burton Tremaine and boats and crews traveled, one race was foremost in their minds. "Fishers Island was the center of our sailing activities and the 'Round Island Race on Labor Day weekend was a race that we particularly focused on," said his son Tony. The club's fleet had long been racing around Fishers before Commodore Harris Parsons opened entries to other clubs in 1964. Although only a dozen boats turned up for that first race, the event grew quickly. In the '70s it acquired the nickname "reaching for grinders" because the race often consisted of fast reaches followed by a post-race party on the club lawn featuring king-size grinder sandwiches, washed down by plenty of beer and rum. Given such a reward, it is not surprising that some participants could act a little goofy, like the crew of Reyn du Pont's *Alinda II* who at one finish surprised the race committee by leaping out from behind the genoa jib in a state of full streaking undress.

Peter Brinckerhoff's Hooligan *makes the most of light air during the 2003 Block Island Race Week. One of the club's most competitive boats of the 1990s, this 42-foot Bob Evelyn design always placed high, whether in the Off Soundings, 'Round Island or Block Island races. In 2003,* Hooligan *won the Harris trophy for the fifth time as the top Fishers boat in the 'Round Island Race.* Tim Wilkes photo

With a typical fleet of more than 60 entries in six classes and a post-race party for several hundred thirsty sailors to host, the 'Round Island Race annually presented the club with serious logistical challenges. For many years, Wally Herrick, Marilyn Porter, and the club's other race committee people ran the starts and finishes, while ashore, the Ladies' Auxiliary managed the drinks and sandwiches until the late 1980s, when the club hired bartenders and served Steve Malinowski's Fishers Island oysters. Twice during the 1990s the Fishers Island Yacht Club was awarded the coveted prize for the best party on the Eastern Connecticut Sailing Association race circuit.

In 1969, in honor of Commodore David F. Harris, a watercolor by Charlie Ferguson was established as the prize for the top Fishers Island boat. After *Chrisada* won it, Eliot Porter rededicated it as a perpetual award in Harris's honor. *Chrisada* won it six times, a Tremaine-owned *Kachina* eight.

Burgees and Uniforms

Except for the observance of Colors, rituals remained foreign to this self-consciously informal yacht club until Commodore Porter instituted a full commissioning, opening-day ceremony, featuring a blessing of the fleet by The Reverend Arthur Lee Kinsolving that is still used today.

In 1974 Commodore Tremaine, Porter's successor, took ceremony to a new level when he bought himself an official blazer, complete with burgee on the pocket, flag officer's stars, and trefoils. Tremaine must have had second thoughts, or maybe he was wary of teasing or criticism, for he did not get around to announcing his acquisition to his fellow flag officers until mid-April. Even then he was cautious. "Perhaps it is being somewhat presumptuous for our low-key club," he wrote, "but I have taken the plunge and have acquired a Commodore's jacket." He advised the other officers that if they thought "this is a little too much, as well they might," they could satisfy him by placing a burgee and stars appropriate for their rank on the pockets of their usual blazers. There is no record of a written reply, but the idea of a little formality became contagious and in 1976 the club arranged for its first official yacht club tie.

The Reverend Arthur Kinsolving delivers the prayer at the club's 1972 commissioning ceremony. Courtesy Sara Porter

As we have already seen in his comments on the 1938 hurricane, Arthur Kinsolving was no fire-and-brimstone preacher. As the opening-day prayer that he wrote in 1972 demonstrates, he even declined an opportunity to call down judgment upon the powerboaters.

Infinite Spirit of God, who through the ages has called men to put to sea, that they may learn of the mysteries, wonders, and terrors of the deep, we thank thee that the lure of the sea reaches us in our time.

We pray it may grow upon us. Though our yacht club depends especially upon motor yachts, we would pray that our young seek, rather than the dizzy joys of speed, the deep satisfaction of sail.

We pray for the ever-widening confraternity in America of those who seek their recreation in the great waters that they may ever discern thy presiding presence as have so many of their forbears.

More especially, we now pray our blessing upon this fleet, upon every ship as we severally embark on the joyous and dangerous adventures of another summer. Bless those who handle them, that they may do so wisely, and with respect for thee, for, O Lord, thy sea is so great, and my ship is so small. AMEN

Peter Sanger

Raised in summers on the Island, Peter Sanger served as a sailing master for the junior program and in the early 1970s took over Pirate's Cove Marine, the Island's only boatyard and marine supply store. He and his wife, Kandi, a daughter of Reynolds du Pont, settled at Fishers fulltime. An enthusiastic sailor who enjoyed owning challenging boats—including Windsurfers and a clipper-bowed schooner called *Sapphire* that he often raced successfully in the annual schooner race sponsored by Mystic Seaport—Sanger also was one of the club's most energetic volunteers. He served as secretary-treasurer and sailing instructor, and provided free winter storage for the club's Boston Whaler and electronic instruments.

In 1980, Pirate's Cove began management of the yacht club piers and floats. Sanger improved launch service, nurtured reciprocity relationships with other clubs, and generally built up the yacht club's spirits. "Everybody rejoiced when Peter took over in 1980," says Sarah W. Rose, a yacht club dockmaster (later its first woman commodore). "He was so instrumental in getting the institution back in order. He got the launch boys back in uniform and got them to do Colors in the morning and at sunset. He got the yacht club back running as a yacht club."

(Left) *Peter and Kandi Sanger.* Courtesy W. Frank Bohlen

(Above) *Heir to the schooner traditions of the club, Peter Sanger's schooner* Sapphire *ghosts along with a large spread of sail.* Courtesy Christopher Sanger

After Peter Sanger's tragic death in an airplane accident in 1986, Chip du Pont, his brother-in-law, took over Pirate's Cove. A self-described "throttle jockey" who, as a boy, was enamored of *Aphrodite* and the other commuters, he spent his spare time in powerboats. As the club's commodore in the early 1980s, the head of Pirate's Cove, the marina's manager, and a member of the Fishers Island Development Company's board of governors, he was involved in an intensifying debate over West Harbor and its uses. In time, concerns about the cleanliness of the water (accentuated by Steve Malinowski's successful development of oyster beds in the harbor) led to the first restrictions on the number and placement of moorings.

The Joys of the Cruising Life

Fishers sailing is hardly all about racing—or even sailing, for that matter. Cruising and fishing in catboats were kings back in the days of George Bartlett, before the arrival of the first small powerboats. For many years, the new yacht club held an annual overnight cruise that bonded all members in all types of boats, large and small. L-16s, H-23s, and other day boats ventured out in company with the schooners, and even *Barlovento* and *Bolero*. After a long absence, the annual cruise was revived in the late 1990s by Commodore Steve Cook, with International One Designs joining the club's cruising fleet of a dozen boats and sailors of all ages on overnight trips to Block or Shelter Island.

Among the club's dedicated recent cruisers was Commodore Bruce May. After coming to Fishers in 1946, he did some racing but was disappointed. "A returning Army veteran found it hard to get excited about who won a sailboat race." He discovered the joys of cruising that August on the first postwar yacht club cruise to Shelter Island, Montauk Pond,

Frank and Elisabeth Bohlen's Ohlson 38 yawl Tattler *represents the club in Off Soundings and has carried the burgee on deepwater races and cruises as far as Newfoundland and Labrador.* Photo by Ted Kelley, Photo-Boat

(Above) *After a cruise to the eastward around 1980, the Bohlen crew of Megan, Anne, Frank, Susan, and Christopher disembarks at the island.* Courtesy W. Frank Bohlen

(Right) *Resurrected in the 1990s, the Fishers Island Yacht Club cruise typically lasts one or two nights, and in 2001, brought a large group of members on sail and powerboats to Shelter Island, New York.* Courtesy Fishers Island Yacht Club

and then home to West Harbor. "On the third day the wind was too strong for the small boats so they were towed home, and I sailed in Pete du Pont's schooner *Barlovento*. That was the first time I ever handled a large, substantial boat, and it was a thrill I remember vividly today, 57 years later." While he never did acquire a *Barlovento*, over the years he had a number of overnighters and small cruising boats, culminating in his Niagara 35 *Scout*.

Another full-time cruising sailor is Gus Kinsolving. In 2003 he looked back on the career of *Seabird*, his Ted Hood-designed 36-foot cruising sloop, which Gus believes was the senior-most boat in the club's fleet 31 years after he first put her on a mooring installed by Ed Hedge. "Dinky Edwards, Monique, and I first sailed *Seabird* to the FIDCO dock at West Harbor in May of 1973. I'd bought her from her first owner, Thomas R. Young, in Greenwich, Connecticut. Built in 1961, she had been named *Shearwater* by him and raced with distinction under that name. Because I had to buy *Shearwater* less her name, I renamed her *Seabird* as the closest I could get to her original, and also in honor of Holling C. Holling's wonderful book of that name, published about 1948 and part of my boyhood. For the next five years, until Isabelle was born, *Seabird* sailed all year 'round out of Fishers and Mystic and did at least three summer cruises to Penobscot Bay, Maine."

Escaping the Doldrums

Despite the dedication to cruising, the success of traveling Bullseye sailors, and the crowds that flocked to the 'Round Island Race, sailing felt becalmed in the 1970s and early '80s as islanders flocked to golf courses and powerboats. There was widespread sentiment that the club needed a new racing boat. Burton Tremaine proposed racing Sunfish, a boat that many families owned, but the idea died on the vine. His successors, Jerry Riegel, Bill Glendon, David Burnham, and Chip du Pont, each struggled in his own way to light a fire. Du Pont recalled, "The club wasn't going to die. There just wasn't much cooking."

In 1983 the club had fewer than 100 members. According to Bruce May, when he became commodore in 1984, "I was appalled and disappointed that with an Island location and one of the great natural harbors on the East Coast, there was so little interest in boating." May quickly made membership easier by replacing an intricate dues system with a flat fee of $80 per family. He also added formality to the opening-day ceremonies and introduced a mid-season social gathering, the Commodore's Reception, offering entertainment for the entire family. May recalls the first reception: "Rear Commodore Sandy Riegel and I secured a marvelous film from Mystic Seaport to show, and we put out the word. After refreshments we set up the projector and screen on the front lawn, but halfway into the film a gust of wind blew the screen down. There was no damage, but some chagrin. We set up again, ran the movie, and all went well." Later, Commodore Laurie Rubinow introduced both a formal Club Night in August and a midwinter gathering at the New York Yacht Club.

Sara Porter sails her Weasel at Hay Harbor around 1962. Courtesy Sara Porter

A New Junior Program

Further brightening the outlook were two developments that picked up on Eliot Porter's challenges. First came a revitalized junior program, then the arrival of a new adult racing class.

In the 1960s and early '70s, junior sailing wasn't much different than it had been in the 1930s. Many younger children still learned basic sailing in a clunky catboat over at the Hay Harbor Club, only now that boat was the Weasel. Juniors who were ambitious to go beyond basic sailing shifted over to West Harbor to sail Bullseyes. They were supervised by a sailing master who ran races and was available to provide instruction on an individual basis. This old system was not succeeding. Young sailors were dropping out, despite the efforts of the sailing masters, who included Tom du Pont, Peter Rugg, Peter Sanger, Ed Heyniger, Geoff Hogan and John, Louise, and Steve Burnham. (When kids did not turn up for lessons, Sanger was known to hunt them down and haul them to the water.) The fact was that the instructors themselves were not happy with the system. Some were bored stiff by having to do individual instruction; all believed that the Bullseye and its usual race courses must be replaced. Children, they urged, should have livelier boats and livelier programs shaped to their interests, not their parents'.

In the early 1970s, the Hay Harbor Club took two steps in a new direction when it replaced the old Weasel with the Widgeon, a small centerboard sloop, and the two clubs began to share instructors and administration of sailing programs. The Bullseye remained important to the junior program. In 1977 sailing master John Burnham rekindled the spirit of the old junior overnight cruises by leading Bullseyes and their young crews off on a voyage to Ocean Beach. Just as the big fleet was clearing West Harbor, a 40-knot thunder squall blew in and swamped the boats. One boat lost its rig and sails entirely (yet went on that year to win a Bullseye Nationals). On another boat, a lightning bolt hit the mast, passed clean through Michael Thatcher, and blew a tiny hole in the hull, fortunately without harming either the skipper or his boat. The worst damage came when anxious parents raced out in powerboats and discovered beer cans floating in the Bullseye bilges. As a result of that small scandal, Burnham ruefully reported, "There's been no junior cruise since."

Despite that hitch, the junior program grew rapidly. Its success was in large part due to a sustained effort on the part of parents and instructors to offer boats and programs that would be good platforms for instruction, while challenging youngsters and providing a standard boat for interclub competition. The first boat of choice was the Blue Jay. Slightly larger than the Widgeon and long popular on the mainland and Long Island Sound, this Sparkman & Stephens class was introduced to the Island when the William Musser family donated a boat to the club in 1984. Before long there were enough privately owned Blue Jays to be used in Wednesday junior races, ending the Bullseye's run as the primary junior boat after more than 50 years.

The junior program took another leap ahead in 1985 when Peter Rugg (a future club commodore) developed a new plan based in part on his boyhood experience at another yacht club, and in part on what he knew about other sail training programs. As he explains, "I began to hatch this scheme: teach the little ones at Hay Harbor and then move them over to bigger boats at the yacht club in steps. One key was to get the boards of both clubs to allow yacht club-member children to participate at Hay Harbor, and vice-versa." That approval was forthcoming.

Essential to this scheme was having not just one suitable boat, but three or four. Like the yacht club's founders back in the 1930s, Rugg believed that each age group should have its own class. A three-tiered system was in place in the summer of 1988. Beginners and girls and boys between 8 and 12 sailed the Optimist. The standard youth training boat in America and abroad, it cost less than $1,300 new and had a large second-hand market. Optimists soon covered the floats at Hay Harbor. At the yacht club, meanwhile, the 11-15-year-old group sailed Blue Jays while older boys and girls interested in racing had a choice between two high-performance 14-foot dinghies, the Laser and the Club 420 (a structurally beefed-up version of a popular international racing class).

The new approach proved extremely successful. Fishers Island soon developed the largest junior sailing program in the Eastern Connecticut Sailing Association, with as many as 160 young sailors taught by four instructors.

Another element of Rugg's plan was that the yacht club would run races for sailors from other clubs. "You've got to be ready to host regattas," he says. "That's what kids want." Commodore Sandy Riegel held the first Fishers Island Junior Regatta in 1987, and under his successor, Peter Rugg, it became an annual event. The club also hosted regional championships for the International 420 Class. Over time, the yacht club's junior program became more closely integrated with Hay Harbor; the first sailing director for the entire Island was hired in 2003.

Beginning in the late 1990s, the yacht club began upgrading its boats for instruction. First it acquired new chase boats; then in 2000 and 2001 it purchased a total of eight 420s not just for junior instruction, but to provide lessons for adults, too. As Commodore Walter Keenan summarized the new outreach policy as a recruiting tool for the club: "We want to have more people enter the sport and having club boats makes it easier."

(Left to right): Beginning in the 80's the club began hosting regattas in International and Club 420s (opposite page) and Optimist Dinghies (above left) and Blue Jays (not shown). Progressively bigger floats housed racing Optimists and eight club-owned 420s by 2002. Courtesy (left to right) Betty Anne Rubinow, John Rousmaniere, Beth Scholle, John Rousmaniere

The popular new class at Hay Harbor is the International Optimist Dinghy, a simple pram that is safe and fun for beginning sailors whether solo or with crew.

Jennifer Parsons photo

FIST

The energetic new junior sailing program turned out a large number of talented sailors who formed the Fishers Island Sailing Team. With their incongruously aggressive FIST logo, the boys and girls traveled to regattas on the mainland and hosted team races with other yacht clubs. Out of that group came several star intercollegiate and Olympic Class sailors, including Brad Gibbs, Arthur Kinsolving, Elizabeth McCance, Dan Rosenthal, and Isabelle Kinsolving.

Courtesy John Rousmaniere

Isabelle Kinsolving became the first Fishers Islander on an Olympic sailing team in 2004, when (with Katie McDowell) she qualified to represent the United States in the women's 470 competition in Athens. When she reflected on her young life in boats, she began with her first sails with her father, Gus, in the family cruising boat and her grandmother, Mary Kinsolving (the widow of The Rev. Arthur Lee), in her Bullseye. At age seven, she started sailing classes at Hay Harbor and eventually worked her way up to 420s. Each summer there would be a trip to the mainland for a regatta and a racing clinic.

The pressure to win from parents and instructors was light. "Once I got through basic sailing I think the primary emphasis was always on fleet racing with a huge focus on having fun. When my friends and I were in Club 420s we had a fantastic instructor, Josh Nadel, who had us focus exclusively on team racing for one summer. FIST (which our instructors, Tanya Haddad, Josh Nadel, and Mike McNamara founded with us) won the ECSA team racing, which made us all inordinately proud." Isabelle went on to sail at Yale, and her success there encouraged her to try out for a position on the Olympic sailing team.

"If children love sailing they will want to become great sailors," noted Isabelle Kinsolving (right). Having grown up cruising with her family and learning to compete in the Island sailing programs, she became a star intercollegiate sailor at Yale and, with Katie McDowell (left), was prepared to represent the U.S. in 470 competition at the 2004 Olympics in Greece.

John Rousmaniere photo. Courtesy John Rousmaniere

"I'd say Fishers best prepared me by teaching me how to love sailing and be pretty self-sufficient and adventurous." She added, "Some of my best friends are the people that I grew up sailing with. I think that one of the best things about the junior program is to teach kids how to sail and race, but, most important, to provide them with something that they love and can do together and make friends doing. That's why we all sailed instead of playing golf or tennis, and I think that's the best part of junior sailing. If children love sailing they will want to become great sailors."

Hooked!

Since the Native American fishermen who may have inspired Adrian Block's name for the Island, there have always been anglers taking advantage of its providentially appointed location. Much of this activity occurred out of sight of most yacht club members, for fishermen are introverts, even loners. The club found this out in 1991 when, in its new "try-anything" mood, it sponsored a 24-hour fishing tournament. As the commodore of that time, Laurie Rubinow, ruefully recalled, "We had more trophies than we had competitors."

For several years in the 1980s yacht club member Bob Miller traced the seasons of Fishers Island fishing in his gracefully written "On the Hook" columns in the *Gazette*. Here is how he described the start of the 1988 fishing season: "On March 17, the first ospreys were reported to have returned to the Island from their southern wintering grounds. Ospreys feed almost exclusively on fish, and their arrival signals the movement of perch and bass into the shallows of the fresh water ponds, and flounder into the harbors—for most, the beginning of the fishing season."

Then came the stripers. "The catching of sizeable bass was so routine this year as to be unremarkable," Miller reported, estimating that one bass was caught for every five bluefish (compared with a ratio of one per fifty in 1984). Later in the summer came the bluefish, which drew the fishermen to the beaches for surf-casting or to their Whalers or larger boats to go out into the Race. Sometimes schools of blues swarmed into inner West Harbor, herding menhaden against the gas dock. If they were not going out after blues in the Race, some Island fishermen chased tuna and swordfish in the ocean, east of Montauk.

Taking it into deep water, Islander Pat Pendergast displays a tuna he hooked off Montauk. Courtesy Fishers Island Gazette

Not all fishing requires a boat. "Charlie's caught snapper off his front porch," Tim Lawrence says about Charlie Ferguson, who always fishes with dry flies. One packing-up day on Columbus Day, despite a cold nor'easter, Ferguson paused from loading the car, grabbed his rod, and waded out into the Sound for a few casts.

After some disappointments, on his last cast of the season he got one. He described the experience in notes in the *Gazette*: "Into the wind for a final try. Almost dark now. Same cast. Same place. Same bizarre fly. Hooked! Played for half an hour. Beached, measured, and released: a 32-inch striper, estimated weight 20 lbs. For this fly fisherman, that is what light tackle fishing is all about. The proper aesthetics were all present that miserable, awful October evening in the gloaming. One is fortunate to have one or two such experiences in a lifetime."

The International One Design

The search for a new racing fleet went unsatisfied for more than a decade. Ensigns, Solings, Etchells 22s, Watch Hill 15s—all are good boats, and all were tried, considered, and rejected as the Fishers Island Yacht Club's new class largely because none of them had the classically sleek appearance that had been deemed necessary for a Fishers racing class since the Herreshoff boats and the Luders 16 came to West Harbor in the 1920s and '30s. The long search finally ended almost accidentally.

Steve Cook admired a classic 34-foot keelboat, the International One Design. As new IODs were built of fiberglass, interest in wooden boats faded. In 1983 Cook found one at Larchmont with an asking price of only $3,000 and an owner who was under pressure to keep the boat nearby. Cook offered twice as much and soon sailed his new boat (now appropriately named *Pre-Emptive Bid*) up to West Harbor. The next summer, because Cynnie Cook was pregnant, the boat was lying in a cradle at Pirate's Cove when another Island sailor, Boots Parker, took a look, did a double-take, and exclaimed, "What's that? I want one!" Soon the yacht club had a fleet of IODs. Charlie Ferguson and Talcott Stanley would declare, "Boots Parker alone brought great racing back to Fishers Island."

Esther "Boots" Riegel Parker Wright, the sister of Commodores Sandy and Jerry Riegel, grew up sailing Weasels at Hay Harbor,

(Left) Esther "Boots" Riegel Parker Wright races offshore in the 1990 Two-Handed Transatlantic Race. Courtesy Sandy Riegel

(Above) "Boots" Parker's IOD, Bête Noire, *flying a "FIOA" (Fishers Island's Own Army) spinnaker, the emblem flown on many Riegel/du Pont clan boats.* Courtesy Sara Porter

but her eyes were on bigger and better boats. Her father owned handsome powerboats called Blue Hen, but, thanks to her uncle, Pierre du Pont, she decided she was a sailor. "Uncle Pete was the reason I sailed. He had big shoes and I tried to fill them." Yet as much as she loved *Barlovento*, she was not allowed to race on her because she was a girl. So she went her own way, becoming, as she says, "a boat groupie."

When she first laid eyes on the International One Design in Peter Sanger's yard, she recalled the stories that a captain of *Blue Hen* had told her about sailing in *Ranger*, the old America's Cup defender. "I thought the IOD looked just like a small J-boat. I thought that's what a sailboat should look like." She made a bid for

The Jester *team, 2003 IOD world champions, race in the Worlds Qualifying Regatta at Fishers. (Left to right) owners Arthur Kuijpers, Charlie Van Voorhis, Jim Thompson.* Chip Riegel photo

Cook's boat but was turned down. She bought another boat that was in terrible shape, learned how to repair it in marathon tutorials in Maine, and then bought two more IODs that she loaned out and later sold, providing the foundation for the new fleet. Moving on to race a catamaran, she skippered the top women's boat in the Two-Handed Transatlantic Race in 1990. That year, thanks largely to her efforts, seven IODs were racing out of West Harbor. Boots Wright later moved to North Carolina and competed in Combined Driving horse-and-carriage events. She had left sailing behind, for, as she explains, "I like to be competitive in just about everything I do, and it's either sailing or ponies."

"The IODs just happened because of Bootsie's love of the boats," says Peter Rugg, and that love was contagious. When Laurie Rubinow was offered an opportunity to buy a boat in 1986, he gathered a syndicate of five—himself, John Burnham, Marty Gibbs, Peter Rugg, and Beth Scholle—that has since been together for more than 15 years. ("The five of us have been a team longer than most marriages," Rugg quipped in 2002.) Syndicate ownership became popular. Besides spreading the cost of maintaining old wooden boats, a syndicate arrangement guarantees that there will be a racing crew on board every weekend regardless of alternating vacation schedules. These multiple-owner teams also provide a lively, intimate community within the larger communities of class and club. Among the consequences of the spread of the IOD was a longer sailing season. The opening day commissioning ceremony was moved from July 4th back to late June and then, in 1997, to Memorial Day weekend. For the first time in its history the club officially had a three-month season.

All did not go perfectly smoothly with the IODs. Charlie Ferguson tells of winning a Labor Day race in *Duchess*, a sieve-like boat whose pump was not up to the job. "We were in second place when the boat started to leak, and then the pump broke. The more water we had, the faster we went. We won the race, took her in, and she sank." *Duchess*, now owned by Chip Flower, is sailing again and most IODs have held up to the strains of racing. While some Fishers IODs are fiberglass, most are wooden and have undergone one degree or another of restoration with the assistance of John Evans, the club's manager, and members like Tim Patterson, Bill Martling, Jim Thompson Jr., Bill Reed and Kevin Farrar. Close competition is maintained by a policy of scheduled purchases of sails of the same design from the same sailmaker for the entire fleet.

In 1996, ten IODs (five of them syndicate-owned) were sailing 30 races a summer. "The IOD became the energy within the club,"

said John Burnham. Much of that energy went into racing, but alternate activities, like crew and novice races, kept the IOD community from becoming too serious about competition. The class fleet captain in the late 1980s, Susan Peabody, not only married one of her competitors, Walter Keenan, but appointed him as her successor.

Formally or informally, IODs offer exciting racing action. Here, Sirius *(#35) and* Norwegian Wood *(#50) reach past Stanley's Beach.* Yves Parent photo. Courtesy Yves Parent

As the IOD fleet expanded to 15 boats, it became increasingly competitive with the *Creole* syndicate (led by Brad Gibbs and Walter Keenan) and the *Kahoutec* syndicate (Kevin Farrar and Thad Cook) joining the fight for the season championship. Racing off-island, Brad Burnham III's *Sirius* team won the 1991 North American Invitational, and after a seventh at their initial world championship in 1988, the *Norwegian Wood* team, with John Burnham at the helm, climbed up to win the 1994 Worlds at Northeast Harbor, Maine, and repeated two years later at Fishers in the first international championship ever held at the Island. The *Jester* team, with Charlie Van Voorhis steering, won the Island's third Worlds title at Northeast Harbor in 2003. (For a summary of Fishers finish results in major championships, see Appendix 2.)

(Top) The Norwegian Wood *team: Marty Gibbs, Peter Rugg, John Burnham, Beth Scholle, and Laurie Rubinow.* Courtesy Fishers Island Gazette

(Above) Norwegian Wood *off the wind on a thick day.* Courtesy John Burnham

"This is a Team Sport"

After the *Norwegian Wood* team won their second International One Design World Championship, at Fishers in 1996, helmsman John Burnham wrote a fond, humorous appreciation of his crew:

Although we really enjoy winning, the silverware is not what motivates us in the first place. It's the process. The experience of an extremely mental and physical game, the character of which changes dramatically depending on whether you're drifting in a wisp of a thermal summer breeze or pounding through large waves in a raw nor'easter of 20 knots or more. On top of that is the fact that, in our International One Design class boats, this is a team sport, which requires coordination, communication, initiative, alertness, and intense concentration.

Well, anyone who knows Peter Rugg knows his jokes are terrible. And that Marty Gibbs has a cell phone attached to his right hip. They know that Beth Scholle is guaranteed to show up fifteen minutes late. And that Laurie Rubinow will come so well prepared that it will take two of us to lift his seabag into the club launch. But, somehow, once we get aboard our boat, the five of us are a team that has learned to work together successfully over the course of nine summers of joint boat ownership.... I'll just tell you (when they're not listening) that they are an extraordinary group of sailors, and that without their commitment and effort, along with the push we've had week after week from the rest of our growing Fishers Island fleet, I wouldn't be writing this article now.

Facing the open Atlantic, Isabella Beach is swathed in storm surf. Courtesy Sara Porter

Yet More Storms and Wrecks

The decade-long hurricane season of the 1950s would not be matched in the late twentieth century, but storms did keep coming. Hurricane Gloria tore up the Island in 1985, but it was almost forgotten six years later in a rare August hurricane, Bob. The high salt spray defoliated the windward sides of the maple trees and left the leeward sides in full fall foliage. The storm threw at least seven boats on West Harbor's shore. The International One Design fleet was badly hit. John Brim's *Flicker* broke from her mooring and ran up on the Peninsula. Peter Rugg, whose Bullseye went on the rocks, estimated *Flicker*'s progress: "Eyewitnesses can attest to the fact that an IOD can move at about 5 knots on a beam reach under bare poles with no one aboard when it is blowing about 90 knots." Two other IODs were rammed by drifting powerboats, and another boat's mooring snapped (though, curiously enough, it was not in the storm but three weeks later).

Nor'easters are more common than hurricanes. A year after Bob, a winter storm submerged Dock Beach and the yacht club docks for three days. A stranger, if happier tale concerns the great blizzard of February 6-7, 1978, known as "the white hurricane." Lance Elwell and Wesley Greenleaf were on their daily afternoon commute to Noank from their jobs at Pirate's Cove when the engine of their 17-foot Whaler quit. They drifted and bailed for 19 hours before fetching up on a Long Island beach. A flight of stairs led to a vacant house, which they broke into. There they discovered that the owner was a man they had known at Fishers.

Fishers Island's long history as a home of shipwrecks did not end with the arrival of radar and satellite navigation. Mariners continued to make dumb mistakes. In August 1988, a cabin cruiser ran up on Race Point at full throttle (her speed was later calculated at 28 knots) and kept going up the shore until she jammed between two boulders. "We heard a loud crash, and then five to ten seconds of engines whining out of the water," said one of the startled onlookers, Tony Redmond. The crew, who suffered only minor injuries, blamed everything on a faulty compass. Six days later, a 400-foot freighter with the less than accurate name *Securitas* ran onto a shoal near Race Point. After she backed off on the rising tide, the Coast Guard investigator, Robert Mott, reported that there had been no mechanical problems. "That leaves only personal error," he went on matter of factly. "You can take it from there."

(Left) *This cabin cruiser beached itself on Race Point in 1988.* (Above) *Hurricane Bob left several boats stranded in the trees, including Bruce May's* Scout *(below) in silver Eel Pond.* Courtesy Sara Porter

John Evans steers the club launch, Attentive, *with Chip Flower aboard, as they approach the club in 2002.* John Rousmaniere photo. Courtesy John Rousmaniere

Expansion in the New Century

The expansion of both the racing schedule and the junior program during the late 1980s and early 1990s stimulated a boom of interest in the yacht club. Membership grew by an average of 30 families a year, rising to 240 members in 1995 and in 2003 reaching a new record of 333.

The club, meanwhile, attempted once again to gain more control of its facility. Almost 50 years earlier, it had bought the land and marina, but with unsatisfactory results. This time the strategy was different: a long-term lease instead of an outright purchase. After lengthy negotiations with the Fishers Island Development Company by Commodores Steve Cook and Sarah Rose and Rear Commodore John Brim, the club revised its agreement to provide for a five-year lease, later extended to ten-year renewable terms. Sarah Rose expressed the aim succinctly: "We wanted FIDCO to give the yacht club back to the yacht club."

Taking control of the marina and its anchorage, and leaving Pirate's Cove Marina to manage rental moorings, the club in 1997 hired a manager with extensive experience with marinas. John Evans, a transplanted Englishman, had sailed a boat to America in the early 1970s and later managed the marina at Mystic Shipyard. "It's a very unpretentious club with some very good sailors," he says of Fishers. "It's a very informal club, and very much a sailing club. For a place like Fishers Island, I had expected it to be a lot stuffier than it is. People are very pleasantly surprised when they get here, and are also surprised by the beauty of the place."

The new arrangement concerning the club facility had immediate positive effects. The budget not only was balanced, but there was a surplus for club improvements. Under Commodores John Brim, Walter Keenan, and Bill Reed, the club acquired Club 420s and supporting powerboats for the sailing program, enlarged the marina, commissioned a club history, and bought a new race committee boat. No doubt the "good fairies" would always be around to chip in funds, but in its 75th anniversary year of 2003,

Walter Keenan's Sparkman & Stephens 55 Southerly *dresses up the club pier in 2003.*

John Rousmaniere photo

John Brim's 60-foot Bruce Farr design Rima *races in the 2003 Sail for Hope in Rhode Island.*

Billy Black photo

the Fishers Island Yacht Club was self-sufficient and considering even further expansion of its programs and facility.

All this time, the past was constantly surfacing—and pleasantly, too. Many members and officers were second- or third-generation Islanders. Former club boats kept appearing, for example, when Bill Hubbard's old Rhodes 27 arrived one day, looking (like the club itself) as crisp and sturdy as she had in the 1930s. On a breezy August Saturday in 2003, half a dozen Fishers Island One Designs sailed over from Groton Long Point, worked their way around the fleets of International One Designs and Bullseyes that were battling off the Dumplings, and dropped anchor near the club's marina so their crews could go ashore to a celebratory party. None of this inspired special notice; the three classes have been prominently racing at or near Fishers over a cumulative period of almost 190 years.

Sailing at Fishers dates back so far —almost four centuries to Adrian Block— that it can never claim to be new. Somehow it does not seem old, either, but as fresh and joyful as its sailors can make it.

Winners of the end-of-season events gather in front of the clubhouse on Labor Day in 2003, having just received their awards. Included are three important trophies for juniors, the Gordon S. Murphy Memorial Trophy (love of sailing), Arthur Lee Kinsolving Trophy (sportsmanship), and Meredith and Peter Rugg Trophy (best at annual Junior Regatta). Courtesy Jennifer Parsons

The Commodore's Cup

The club's turn into the new millennium has seen achievements that, in their own way, are as noteworthy as those of the yacht club's famous earlier eras, when *Barlovento, Aphrodite, Bolero,* and other classic yachts were moored in West Harbor, and when the club's name was carried by classes designed by Nat Herreshoff and other fine naval architects. In the two-year period 2002-03, Isabelle Kinsolving qualified for the U.S. Olympic Team, Charlie van Voorhis won the International One Design World Championship, Peter Rugg won a Bullseye National Championship and was on the winning doublehanded boat in the Newport-Bermuda Race, David Burnham won a Bullseye nationals with a perfect score, and John Brim and Sara Porter and Geordie Loveday were regularly winning silver in long-distance and Off Soundings Club events.

The club's long tradition of achievement was honored by the creation of a new club trophy, the Commodore's Cup, at the instigation of board member Jennifer Mancusi-Ungaro and her husband Greg. The Cup (to quote its citation) "honors a member of the Club who has attained an outstanding achievement or competitive result in the field of Yachting during the preceding year."

In 2001 Commodore Brim presented the Commodore's Cup to long time club governor Frank Bohlen for navigating the Mystic Seaport schooner *Brilliant* to a 1st in class and 1st overall victory in the Tall Ships 2000 Transatlantic Race. In 2002 Commodore Keenan presented it to Peter Rugg, and in 2003 Dave Burnham was awarded the cup by Keenan in part for his victory in the Bullseye nationals, in part for his lifetime of sailing achievement.

COMMODORE

1928-32, Arthur E. Whitney
1933-36, Franklin M. Haines
1937-38, Arthur E. Whitney
1939-41, Thomas W. Russell
1942-46, William H. Hubbard
1947-48, John Nicholas Brown
1949-58, Pierre S. du Pont III
1959-61, Reynolds du Pont
1962-64, Harris B. Parsons
1965-67, Talcott Stanley
1968-69, David H. Harris
1970-71, Michael Laughlin
1972-73, Eliot H. Porter II
1974-75, Burton G. Tremaine Jr.
1976-77, Richard E. Riegel Jr.
1978-79, William H. Glendon
1980-81, David C. Burnham
1982-83, Reynolds du Pont Jr.
1984-85, William B. May Jr.
1986-87, John E. Riegel
1988-90, Peter Rugg
1991-92, Laurence P. Rubinow
1993-94, Stephen A. Cook
1995, Thomas W. Cashel
1996-97, Sarah W. Rose
1998-99, John S. Burnham
2000-01, John G. Brim
2002-03, Walter C. Keenan
2004, William D. Reed

VICE COMMODORE

1931-38, Thomas W. Russell
1939-41, William H. Hubbard
1942, Reynolds du Pont
1943-46, no records
1947, Gordon Murphy
1948, Pierre S. du Pont III
1949-51, Gordon Murphy
1952-54, William H. Hubbard
1955-58, John C. Wilmerding
1959, Pierre S. du Pont III
1960-61, John C. Wilmerding
1962, William B. Campbell
1963-66, William C. Ridgeway III
1967, David H. Harris
1968-69, Michael Laughlin
1970-71, Eliot H. Porter II
1972-73, W. R. Herrick
1974-75, Richard E. Riegel Jr.
1976-77, William H. Glendon
1978-79, David C. Burnham
1980-81, Reynolds du Pont Jr.
1982-83, William B. May Jr.
1984-85, Porter Goss
1986, No Record
1987, Peter Rugg
1988-89, Linda S. Musser
1990, Laurence P. Rubinow
1991-92, Stephen A. Cook
1993-94, Thomas W. Cashel
1995, Sarah W. Rose
1996-97, John S. Burnham
1998-99, John G. Brim
2000-01, Walter C. Keenan
2002-03, William D. Reed
2004, John Stephen McGeeney

REAR COMMODORE

1931-32, Mrs. Henry J. Fuller
1933-35, Charles A. Goodwin
1936-37, Pierre S. du Pont III
1940-41, Reynolds du Pont
1942, Gordon Murphy
1943-46, no record
1947-48, Sanford Simmons
1949-50, Joseph Middlebrook Jr.
1951, John C. Wilmerding
1952, Gordon Murphy
1953-56, Harris B. Parsons
1957, William B. Campbell
1958-59, William C. Ridgeway Jr.
1960-61, G. deF. Lord
1962, William C. Ridgeway III
1963-64, Talcott Stanley
1965-67, Peter D. Sanger
1968-69, Eliot H. Porter II
1970-71, W. R. Herrick
1972-73, Burton G. Tremaine Jr.
1974-75, William H. Glendon
1976-77, David C. Burnham
1978-79, Reynolds du Pont Jr.
1980-83, Porter Goss
1984-85, John E. Riegel
1986, Peter Rugg
1987-89, James Thompson
1990, Stephen A. Cook
1991-92, John S. Burnham
1993, Gordon S. Murphy Jr.
1994, Sarah W. Rose
1995, John S. Burnham
1996-97, John G. Brim
1998-99, Walter C. Keenan
2000-01, William D. Reed
2002-03, John Stephen McGeeney
2004, William J. Fiske

SECRETARY-TREASURER

1928, Thomas W. Russell
1929-36, W. S. Glazier
1937, Marion Utley
1947, Pierre S. du Pont III
1948-58, Reynolds du Pont
1959-61, William C. Ridgeway III
1962-64, Reynolds du Pont
1965-71, Burton G. Tremaine Jr.
1972-83, Peter D. Sanger
1984-87, William B. May Jr.
1988-91, Sarah E. Walsh (Rose)

SECRETARY

1938, Gordon S. Murphy
1939, Francis W. Cole Jr.
1943-46, no records
1991-92, Gordon S. Murphy Jr.
1993-97, Jennifer J. Miller
1998-04, Anne W. Burnham

TREASURER

1938-42, Marion Utley
1943-46, no records
1991-92, Gigi Murphy
1993-95, Stewart L. Cutler
1996-1998, Jeffrey J. Miller
1999-2001, Frances R. Spark
2002-2004, Kevin Grant

FIYC at the Bullseye Nationals, 1975-2003, top 5 finishes.

Since Fishers sailors started attending Bullseye nationals in 1975, they have won 12 of the 29 titles—five by the Rugg family, seven by Burnhams—and finished out of the top five only five times.

1975 Marion, Massachusetts, 21 boats
1st, John Burnham (David & Steve Burnham)

1976 Marblehead, Massachusetts, 20 boats
1st, John Burnham (David & Steve Burnham)

1977 Fishers Island, New York, 26 boats
1st, Steve Burnham (Fred Treffeisen, Sally Lockwood)
2nd, Eliot Porter (Peter Sanger)
3rd, Charlie Ferguson (Frank Bohlen)
5th, William Martling

1978 Rockport, Massachusetts, 23 boats
3rd, Charlie Ferguson (Frank Bohlen)
4th, David Burnham (Paul Burnham, Jay Ward)

1979 Marion, Massachusetts, 19 boats
1st, David Burnham (Paul Burnham, Jay Ward)
4th, Charlie Ferguson (Frank Bohlen)

1980 Padanarum, Massachusetts, 10 boats
1st, David Burnham (William Martling, Paul Burnham)
5th, Charlie Ferguson (Frank Bohlen)

1981 Fishers Island, New York, 21 boats
2nd, Rod Hickey (Steve Burnham, Steve Hencken)
3rd, Geoffrey Hogan (not available)
4th, Charlie Ferguson (Eliot Porter, Lyon Osborne)

1982 Rockport, Massachusetts, 13 boats
4th, David Burnham (Paul and Louise Burnham)

1984 Marion, Massachusetts, 19 boats
2nd, Laurie Rubinow (Steve Burnham)

1985 Rockport, Massachusetts, 19 boats
1st, David Burnham (John Burnham)
2nd, Laurie Rubinow (Steve Burnham)
3rd, Jim Thompson Jr. (Jim Thompson Sr.)

1986 Fishers Island, New York, 24 boats
2nd, Peter Rugg (Peter Mahony)
3rd, Charlie Ferguson (Dave Burnham)
4th, Jim Thompson Jr. (Jim Thompson Sr.)

1987 Marion, Massachusetts, 18 boats
2nd, Laurie Rubinow (Steve Burnham, Rob Scala)
(regatta won by Charlie Van Voorhis representing Mattapoisett YC)

1988 Rockport, Massachusetts, 20 boats
1st, Peter Rugg (Charlton Rugg)
2nd, Laurie Rubinow (Steve Burnham)
3rd, David Burnham (Paul Burnham)
4th, Brad Burnham Jr. (Charlie Van Voorhis)

1989 Key Largo, Florida, 21 boats
3rd, Peter Rugg (Meredith Rugg)

1990 Southwest Harbor, Maine, 32 boats
1st, Peter Rugg (Caroline Rugg)
2nd, David Burnham (Paul Burnham)
3rd, Laurie Rubinow (Steve Burnham)

1991 Fishers Island, New York, 20 boats
2nd, Caroline Rugg (Peter Rugg)

1992 Rockport, Massachusetts, 20 boats
1st, Caroline Rugg (Peter Rugg)
2nd, Jim Thompson Jr. (Jim Thompson Sr.)
4th, David Burnham (Paul Burnham)
5th, Brad Burnham Jr. (Charlie Van Voorhis)

1993 Marion, Massachusetts, 19 boats
3rd, Jim Thompson Jr. (Jim Thompson Sr.)
4th, David Burnham (Paul Burnham)
5th, Brad Burnham Jr. (Charlie Van Voorhis)

1995 Southwest Harbor, Maine, 21 boats
5th, David Burnham (Paul Burnham)

1997 Fishers Island, New York, 19 boats
1st, Caroline Rugg/Peter Rugg (co-skippers)
2nd, Jim Thompson Jr. (Jim Thompson Sr.)
5th, Charlie Ferguson (Jennifer Miller)

1999 Rockport, Massachusetts, 14 boats
5th, Brad Burnham Jr. (Charlie & Lyon Van Voorhis)

2000 Key Largo, Florida, 29 boats
2nd, Peter Rugg (Basil Vasiliou)

2002 Fishers Island, New York, 20 boats
1st, Peter Rugg/Caroline Rugg (co-skippers)

2003 Marion, Massachusetts., 24 boats
1st, David Burnham (Steve Burnham, Paul Burnham)

FIYC at the International One Design Class World Championship, top 5 finishes.

After the IOD fleet was established at Fishers Island in 1985, a Fishers team first sailed in the class's world championship in 1988, when the *Norwegian Wood* team finished seventh. Since then, Fishers sailors have won three worlds and finished 10 times in the top five.

1990 Glasgow, Scotland
3rd, *Norwegian Wood* team– John Burnham, Marty Gibbs, Alan McKay, Laurie Rubinow, Peter Rugg

1991 San Francisco, California
4th (tie), *Norwegian Wood* team – John Burnham, Brad Gibbs, Marty Gibbs, Laurie Rubinow, Beth Scholle

1992 Marblehead, Massachusetts
4th, *Norwegian Wood* team – John Burnham, Laurie Rubinow, Meredith Rugg, Peter Rugg, and Mike Breault (Meredith Rugg won the Priscilla Kehm award)

1994 Northeast Harbor, Maine
1st, *Norwegian Wood* team – John Burnham, Brad Burnham, III, Marty Gibbs, Laurie Rubinow, Beth Scholle

1996 Fishers Island, New York
1st, *Norwegian Wood* team – John Burnham, Marty Gibbs, Laurie Rubinow, Peter Rugg, Beth Scholle
4th, *Creole* team – Brad Gibbs, Brian Doyle, Mac Dunwoody, Walter Keenan, Basil Vasiliou

1997 Western Long Island Sound
3rd , *Norwegian Wood* team – John Burnham, Marty Gibbs, Laurie Rubinow, Meredith Rugg, Peter Rugg

1999 San Francisco, California
3rd, *Norwegian Wood* team – John Burnham, Thad Cook, Jeff Feehan, Peter Rugg, Beth Scholle

2000 Sweden
2nd, *Norwegian Wood* team – John Burnham, Laurie Rubinow, Beth Scholle, Ollie Scholle, Peter Rugg

2001 (sailed in 2002), Marblehead, Massachusetts
4th, *Norwegian Wood* team – John Burnham, Marty Gibbs, Laurie Rubinow, Beth Scholle, Ollie Scholle

2003 Northeast Harbor, Maine
1st, *Jester* team – Charles Van Voorhis, Jim Thompson Jr., Chip Johns, Greg Russell, Carolyn Grant
4th, *Norwegian Wood* team – John Burnham, Jennifer Miller, Peter Rugg, Laurie Rubinow, Beth Scholle

North American Championship, Fishers Island victories
1991, Brad Burnham, Jim Hickey, Charlie Van Voorhis

Seven racing classes designed between 1910 and 1939 carried the Fishers Island or Fishers Island Sound names. One was not constructed, while the other six were built for Island sailors at three of America's finest yacht yards—Herreshoff, Nevins, and Luders.

Fishers Island One Design

Although "Fishers Island Yacht Club" is written on the plans for this out-and-out racer, it is the only boat in this group that was not built, at least for Island sailors. It would have been like the fast, flat-bottom bilgeboard scows that are still popular on small lakes, sheltered bays, and other smooth waters. 38' length overall (LOA) bilgeboard scow designed by Charles D. Mower in 1910.

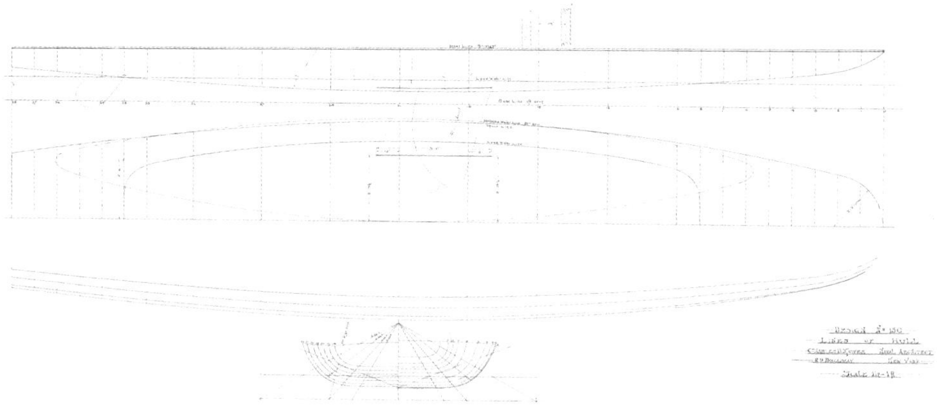

Fishers Island One Design

(also called FIOD, Groton Long Point Class A)

The oldest Fishers boat, the FIOD was the only centerboard class built expecially for the Island. As the Class A, it was still racing on Fishers Island Sound in 2003, 93 years after it was designed. Each year several Class As sail over to West Harbor for a party at the Pequot Inn. 24' LOA, 15' waterline length LWL centerboard daysailer, commissioned by FIYC, designed in 1910 by Charles D. Mower and built by Henry B. Nevins, Inc., City Island, New York, in three groups, in 1910, 1913, and 1922-23. A total of 24 FIODs were raced at one time or another at Fishers from 1910 to 1933, when most were sold to the mainland; a few continued to race through 1937. Many FIODs remain active as the Class As at the Groton Long Point Yacht Club, on the Connecticut shore across from Fishers Island.

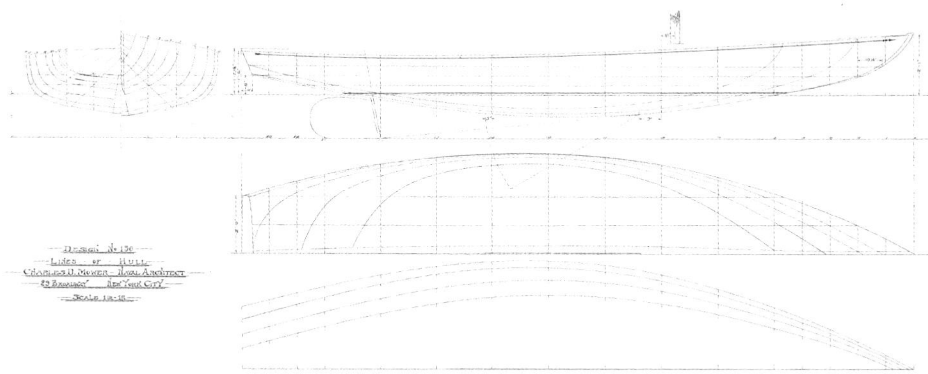

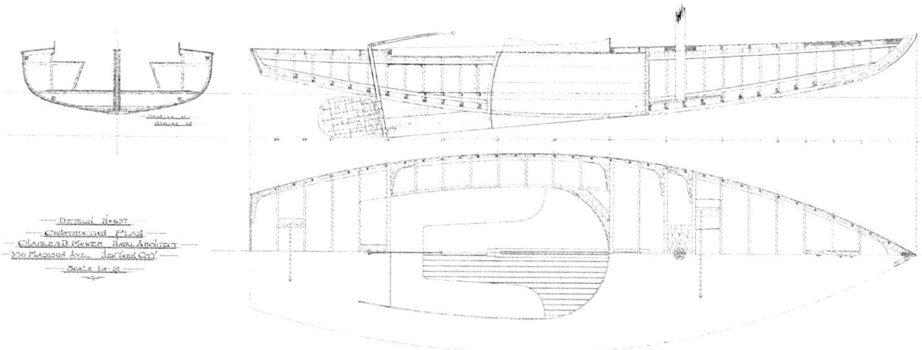

(Above) Ships Plans Library, Mystic Seaport

(Right) Courtesy M. Lee Gaillard

Fishers Island Sound 31

(Fishers Island 31)

Boats in this handsome Herreshoff one-design cruising class were built for several owners on the mainland or Island shores of Fishers Island Sound. It has compiled an excellent record, whether in competition or on long voyages (one completed a circumnavigation). 43' LOA, 31' LWL cruising-racing keel sloop, commissioned by a sailor from Watch Hill, designed in 1927 by A. Sydney De Wolf Herreshoff based on his father Nathanael G. Herreshoff's Newport 29, and built at the Herreshoff Manufacturing Co., Bristol, Rhode Island. Although its official name was the Fishers Island Sound 31 (the insignia read "FIS"), the Herreshoff yard called it the Fishers Island class. Six boats raced at Fishers Island ca. 1928-1935.

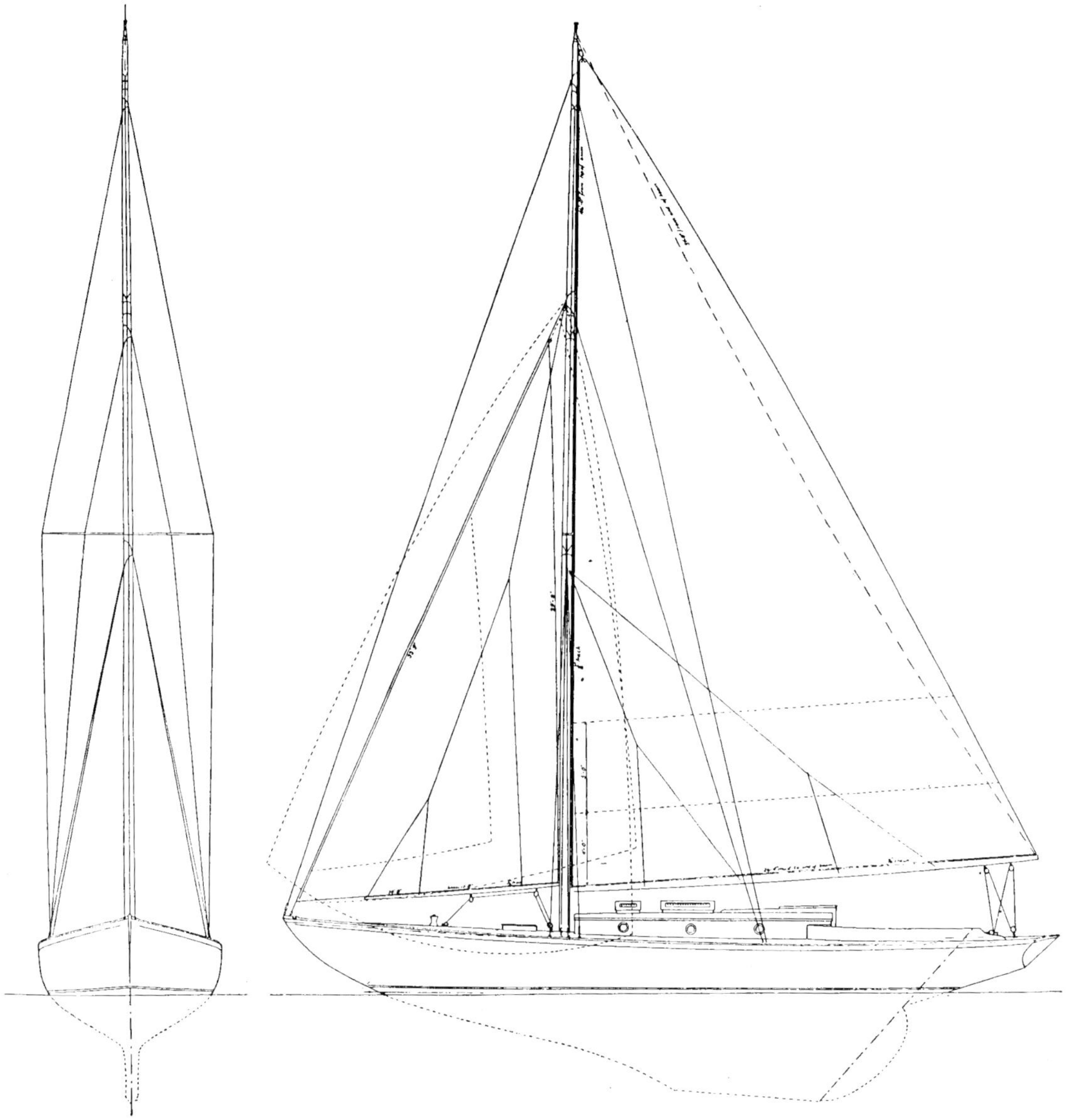

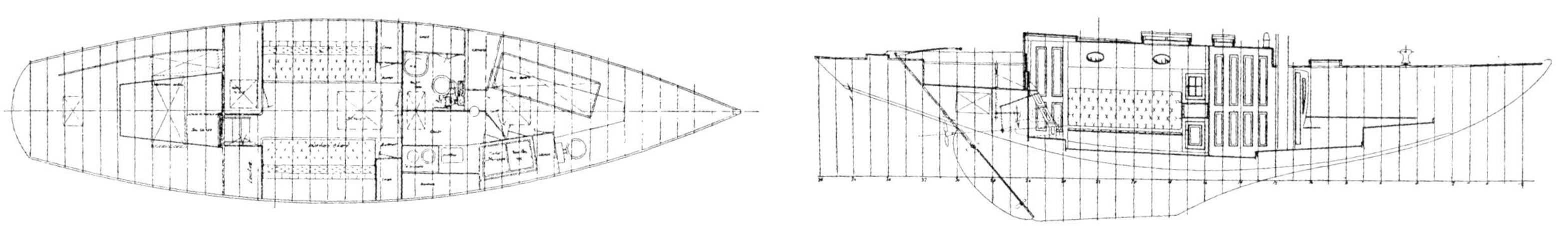

(Above) Herreshoff Marine Museum

(Right) *Kelpie*. Morris Rosenfeld photo. 1984.187.64848F ©Mystic Seaport, Rosenfeld Collection

A full model of a Fishers Island Bullseye serves as the club's H. Lee Ferguson Jr. Trophy, presented by Reynolds du Pont in 1966 and awarded every year since.

Dennis Murphy photo

Fishers Island Bullseye

(Bullseye, Bulls-Eye, etc.)

One of America's classic sailboats, the Bullseye has been raced at Fishers and in New England, Florida, or other areas for more than 75 years, with Fishers Island sailors often winning national championships. 15′10″ LOA, 12′6″ LWL Marconi-rigged sloop developed in 1925 by A. Sidney DeWolf Herreshoff from his father's gaff-rigged Herreshoff 12½, and built in various versions at the following yards: 1925-39, Herreshoff Manufacturing Co., Bristol, Rhode Island; 1939-46, Quincy Adams Yacht Yard, Quincy, Massachusetts; and since 1946 in fiberglass at Cape Cod Shipbuilding Co., Wareham, Massachusetts. Raced continuously at Fishers Island since 1928, first out of Hay Harbor and, after 1938, out of West Harbor, the Bullseye was the Island's primary junior boat until replaced by the Blue Jay in 1985. As many as 25 Bullseyes have been in commission on Fishers in some years.

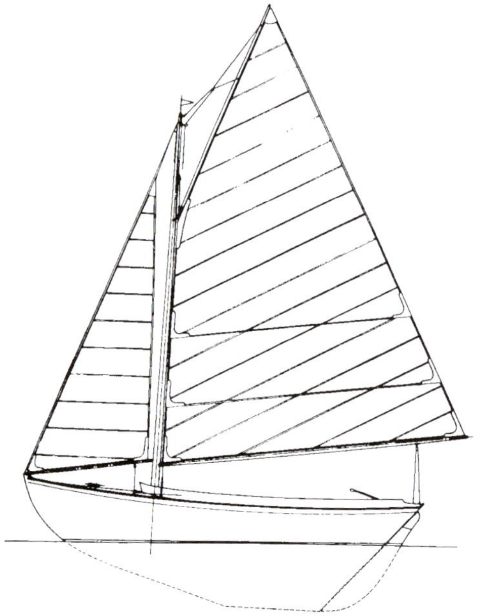

(Left) Herreshoff Bullseye

(Right) Fishers Island Bullseye, Cape Cod Shipbuilding Company

A fleet of Bullseyes get underway during the 1977 Nationals at Fishers.

John Harper photo. Courtesy Dave Burnham

The sleek lines of the Fishers Island 23 are displayed in the Club's Season Championship trophy for that class, awarded between 1932 and 1952.
Dennis Murphy photo

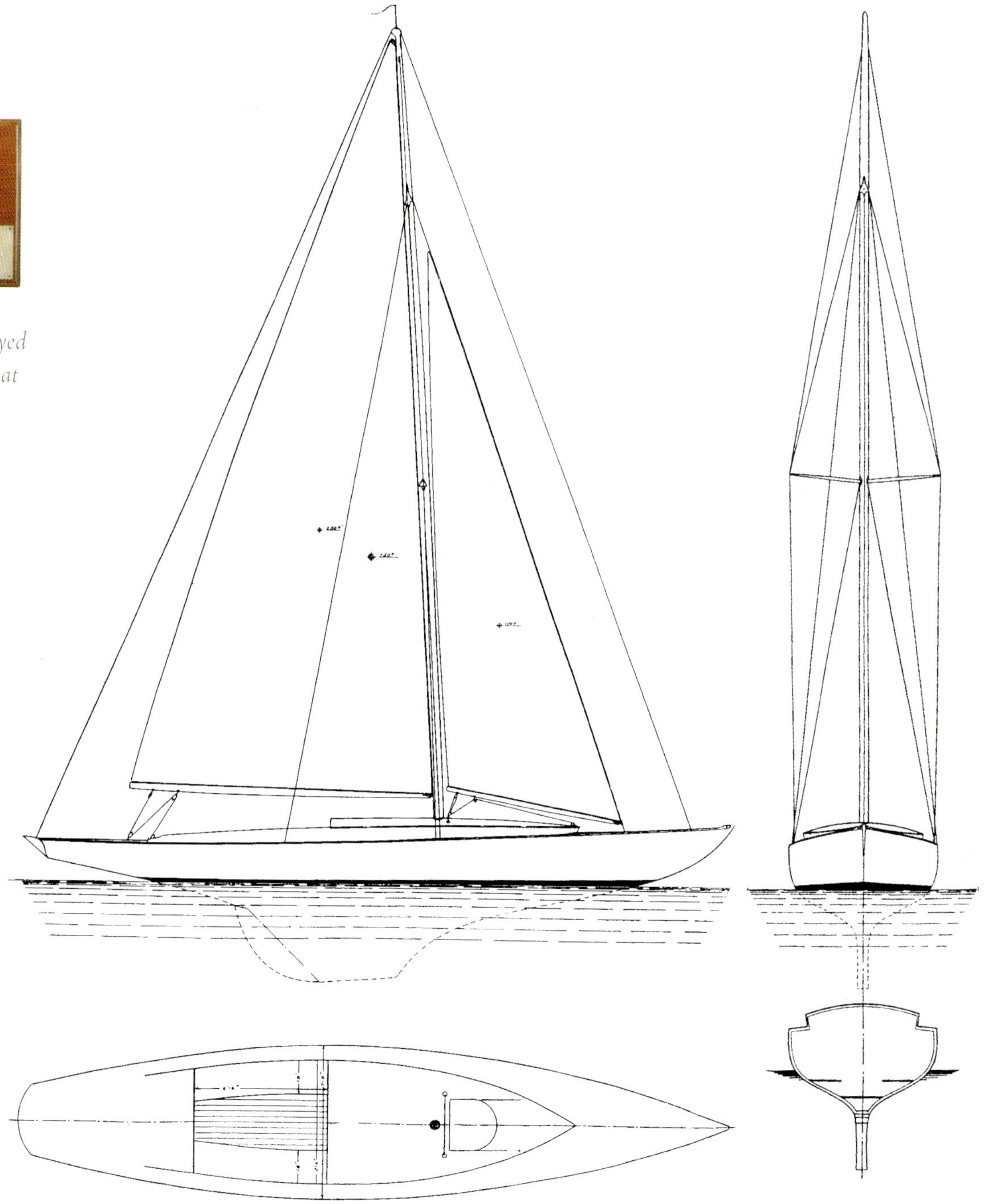

Fishers Island 23

(also Herreshoff 23, H-23)

The third of Fishers' three Herreshoff classes, this attractive racing boat based on a Scandinavian type had limited accommodations for cruising. It was popular in West Harbor for many years. 34' LOA, 23' LWL keel daysailer, commissioned by FIYC, designed by A. Sidney DeWolf Herreshoff in 1932, and built at Herreshoff Manufacturing Co., Bristol, Rhode Island. Raced at Fishers Island 1932-ca. 1955.

(Above) Herreshoff Marine Museum

(Right) Katydid. Morris Rosenfeld photo. 1984.187.69117F ©Mystic Seaport, Rosenfeld Collection

H23
3

The club's Three Year Cruise Trophy for the Rhodes 27 Class, presented by Franklin M. Haines, shows off the lines of this sturdy cruiser and was awarded from 1939 to 1952. Dennis Murphy photo

Rhodes 27

(also Fishers Island Class)

Like the FIS-31, the Rhodes 27 is a cruising boat (though with more expansive and modern accommodations) and has been used for cruising and racing over short and long courses. 39' LOA, 27' LWL cruising-racing sloop, commissioned by FIYC, designed by Philip L. Rhodes, built by Henry B. Nevins, Inc., City Island, New York. Several Rhodes 27s sailed at Fishers 1939-ca. 1955.

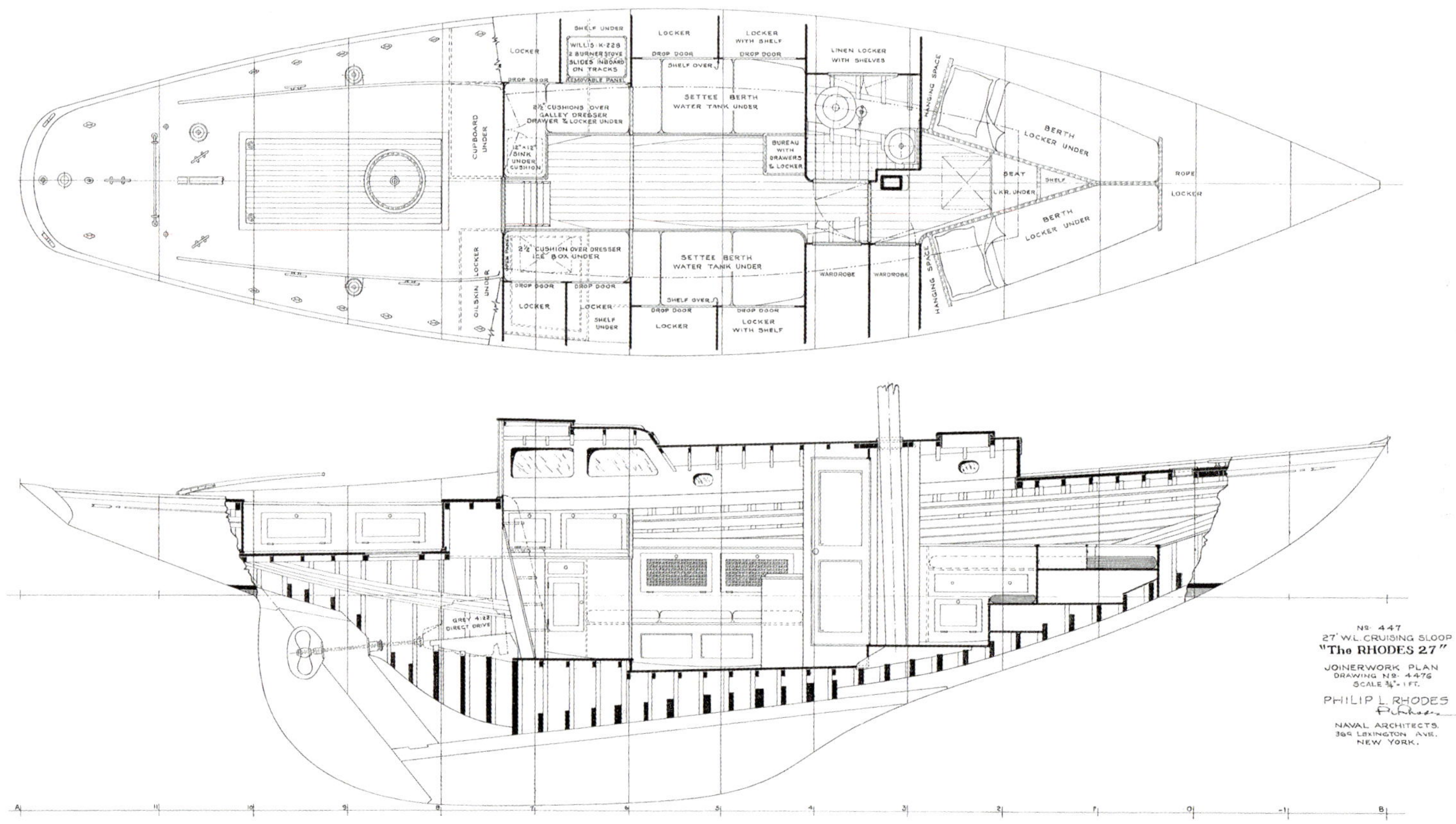

(Above) Ships Plans Library, Mystic Seaport

(Right) T.W. Russell's Savage *daysails along the Fishers Island shore.* Morris Rosenfeld photo. 1984.187.69117F ©Mystic Seaport, Rosenfeld Collection

R27
I

Luders 16

(also L-16, Fishers Island One Design, Fishers Island L Class)

Like the Bullseye, the L-16 has mustered a dedicated following far from Fishers Island, for which it was originally created. 26′4″ LOA 16′4″ LWL keel daysailer, commissioned by FIYC, designed by A.E. Luders, Sr. and Jr., and built of planked construction by the Luders Marine Construction Co., Stamford, Connecticut. A prototype built in 1933 stimulated a fleet order in 1934. A dozen L-16s raced until the 1938 hurricane left only four boats, a few of which continued to sail at Fishers until sold to Niantic, Connecticut. Late, L-16s built of molded plywood or fiberglass were raced in other American waters and in Bermuda. L-16s are now racing at Northeast Harbor, Maine.

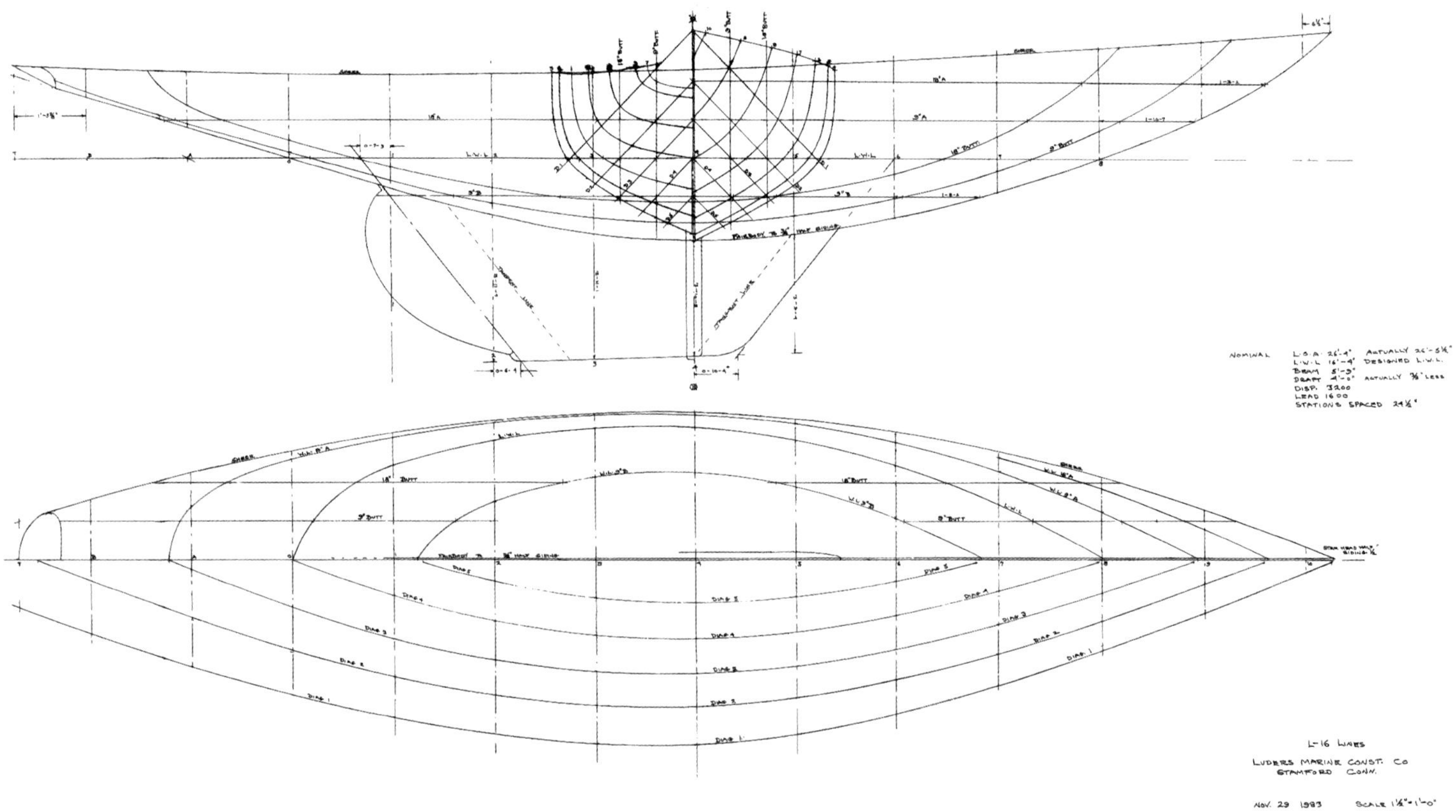

(Above) Ships Plans Library, Mystic Seaport

(Right) The prototype L-16. Courtesy Robert Wallstrom

Author Acknowledgments

I thank first John Burnham and his colleagues on the Fishers Island Yacht Club's History Committee for inviting me to participate in this fascinating project, and then the many people who took the time to talk or write about a place that means so much to them. Pierce Rafferty, curator at the Henry L. Ferguson Museum, has been an enthusiastic, encyclopedic, and essential source of Island history. Dave Burnham, Jim Egan, Charlie Ferguson, Happy Gaillard, Chip du Pont, Sara Porter, and Laurie Rubinow generously provided records, correspondence, news clippings, and other materials.

Every historian owes a debt to the institutions that have collected, preserved, and made available information that most people would consider arcane. The institutions where I conducted research were, on Fishers Island, the Fishers Island Library and Henry L. Ferguson Museum; at Mystic Seaport, the G.W. Blunt White Library, the Rosenfeld Collection, and the Ships Plans Collection; in New London, the New London County Historical Society and Public Library of New London; in New York, the Columbia University libraries, the New York Public Library, and the library of the New York Yacht Club; and in Stamford, Conn., the Ferguson Library.

At Mystic Seaport, Andy German has been a prince among editors–tactful and almost always correct. For permission to quote from publications or correspondence I thank Dave Burnham, Jim Egan, Charlie Ferguson, *The Fishers Island Gazette*, the New London County Historical Society, *The Day* of New London, the Noank Historical Society, and Mystic Seaport.

Sources

Calculations for inflation are from The Inflation Calculator, http://www.westegg.com/inflation/. Yacht Registers used: *The American Yacht List, Manning's Yacht Register, Lloyd's Register of American Yachts.*

Oral Histories, Memoirs, or Interviews

Charles Brainard, John Nicholas Brown III, John Brim, Bradford Burnham Jr., David Burnham, John Burnham, Stephen Burnham, Elizabeth Hubbard Cook, Stephen Cook, Reynolds du Pont Jr., Thomas du Pont, James F.X. Egan, John Evans, Charles B. Ferguson, E. Marie Gaillard, William Glendon, Herbert Grandage, Rodney Johnstone, Susan Peabody Keenan, Walter C. Keenan, Augustus B. Kinsolving, Isabelle Kinsolving, Monique Kinsolving, Timothy Lawrence, Jean McIntire Leuchtenburg, William B. May, Thomas Nye, Harris B. Parsons, Eliot Porter II, Sara H. Porter, Pierce Rafferty, Lisa Cook Reed, William D. Reed, John Riegel, Christopher du P. Roosevelt, Sarah W. Rose, Laurence Rubinow, Peter Rugg, Talcott Stanley, Burton G. Tremaine III, Robert Wallstrom, Esther "Boots" Riegel Parker Wright.

Fishers Island history: Charles B. Ferguson and Pierce Rafferty, *The Fishers Island Club and Golf Links: The First Seventy-Five Years, 1926-2001*, 2nd ed. (Fishers Island: Fishers Island Club, 2002); *Henry L. Ferguson, Fishers Island, N.Y., 1614-1925* (New York: n.p., 1925); F.E. Hine, *Fishers Island: Its History and Development* (n.p., ca. 1925); Pierce Rafferty and John Wilton, *Guardian of the Sound: A Pictorial History of Fort H.G. Wright, Fishers Island, New York* (New York: Fossil Photos, 1998); Henry Robinson Palmer, "Fishers Island, a Former Bit of New England," *New England Magazine* (July 1903): 567-84; James and Joanne Wall, *Fishers Island: A Book of Memories* (Fishers Island: Peninsula Press, 1982).

Most issues of the *Fishers Island Gazette* include at least one article on the Island's history.

Chapter I: "An Entirely Different Climate" – 1614-1900

Early yachting: Arthur H. Clark, *The History of Yachting, 1600-1815* (New York: Putnam's, 1904); John Rousmaniere, *The Golden Pastime: A New History of Yachting* (New York: W.W. Norton, 1987).

Fishers Island Sound hazards: George Fox, http:// bible. christiansunite.com/ geo/geo18.shtml; *The Diary of Joshua Hempstead* (New London: New London County Historical Society, 1999); "Six hours of ebb," John Burnham, program for 1996 International One Design World Championship; *Blunt's American Coast Pilot*, 7th ed. (1809); *Atlantic Local Coast Pilot*, 2nd ed. (1880); *U.S. Coast Pilot, Atlantic Coast* (1918); "baffling winds, calms, and fogs," *New York Times*, August 11, 1867; sperm whale, *New York Tribune*, December 11, 1894.

Lighthouses and navigation aids: Robert G. Banchand, *Northeast Lights* (Norwalk, Conn.: Sea Sports, 1989); Benjamin F. Rathbun, *Capsule Histories of Some Local Islands and Light Houses in the Eastern*

Part of L.I. Sound (Niantic, Conn.: Presley, 1996); F. Hopkinson Smith, *Captain Thomas A. Scott: Master Diver* (Boston: American Unitarian Association, 1908); Charles B. Ferguson, *Twenty-Seven Views of Race Rock Lighthouse in the Four Seasons* (Fishers Island: North Hill Press, 2000); 19 lights visible: *The Day*, September 8, 1881; Money Pond Bay, *Noank: Celebrating a Maritime Heritage* (Noank, Conn.: Noank Historical Society, 2002), 98-99; West Harbor channel, *The Day*, December 14, 1889; 1877 Fishers Island Sound chart at http://chartmaker.ncd.noaa.gov/csdl/ctp/abstract.htm.

Storms and wrecks: surfboatmen endorsement, *Francis' Metallic Life-Boat Company* (New York: W.C. Bryant, 1852); "Hurricane haven," Naval Meteorology and Oceanography Command, "Tropical Cyclones Affecting Groton/New London," http://www.cnmoc.navy.mil/ nmosw/tr8203nc/nlondon/text/sect7.htm; Carol Ridgway, "The Storm of 1717," *Fishers Island Gazette*, November 1991; "The Ever-Memorable September Gale, 1815," R.M. Devens, *American Progress: The Great Events of the Greatest Century* (n.p.: Nichols, 1893), 178-85; "The heart sickens," David M. Ludlum, *Early American Hurricanes, 1492-1870* (Boston: American Meteorological Society, 1963); "Sixty years ago," Ferguson, *Twenty-Seven Views of Race Rock Lighthouse*; Carol Ridgway, "Famous Shipwrecks over the Years," *Fishers Island Gazette*, August 1990; *Atlantic*, Carol Ridgway, "The Tale of the Tolling Bell," *Fishers Island Gazette*, August 1991; "The Loss of the Steamer C. *Vanderbilt*," *Harper's Weekly*, January 22, 1859.

1880s: "The tranquil waters," *Fisher's Island* (New York: Lawrence & Allen, 1875); Lyles Beach, *The Day*, July 9 and 18, 1883, May 27, 1884; prohibition, *Willimantic Chronicle*, June 27, 1883, http://www.geocities.com/Heartland /Fields/4791/ june1883.html; "grand regatta," *New York Times*, July 21, 1884, *The Day*, July 24, 1884.

The first Fishers Island Yacht Club: certificate of incorporation, March 22, 1886, copy in By-Laws file, FIYC Archives; American yacht clubs, Henry H. Anderson Jr. and Robert C. MacArthur, *The Centennial History of the United States Sailing Association* (Newport, R.I.: U.S. Sailing Association, 1997); *Watch Hill Yacht Club, 1913-1963* (n.p., n.d.); Stewart W. Herman, *The Shelter Island Yacht Club: A Centennial History, 1866-1986* (n.p.: n.d)

Catboats: "Almost like a yacht," Howard Burdick, oral history, Mystic Seaport; "It was amazing," William E. Simmons, "When New York Bay was a Yachting Center," *Yachting* (March 1915): 143; "A fine new catboat," *The Day*, July 29, 1896, in *Noank: Celebrating a Maritime Heritage*, 191-92.

Fishers Island in the 1880s and 1890s: correspondence and conversations with Pierce Rafferty and Jim Wall; "It was loaded," *The Day*, June 13, 1884; "I particularly desire," *New York Times*, July 15, 1886; "The place seems to be," *The Day*, June 24, 1889; Gordon S. Murphy, Thomas W. Russell Jr., and Miner H. Warner, *A Short History of St. John's Episcopal Church, Fishers Island, New York* (2003); "Some of the fastest," "one can sit," *Munnatawket Hotel* (1893).

George H. Bartlett: Bartlett, *Water Tramps, or the Cruise of the Sea Bird* (New York: Putnam's, 1895) and *A Commercial Trip with an Uncommercial Ending* (New York: Putnam's, 1884) (both in Lyle H. Wright, *American Fiction*, vol. 3, microfilm, Reel B23, no. 361-62); "successfully gathering roses," R.T. McMullen, *Down Channel* (London, 1869 and subsequent editions).

Chapter II: "It was a Getaway" – 1900-38

West Harbor: "Mr. Ferguson intends," *New London Day*, December 14, 1889; Mary Roberts, "Retrospective: Fishers Island Bricks," *Fishers Island Gazette*, November 1998; "The small boat," Rufus B. Burnham (writing as Bradford Burnham), "Cruising in an Open Launch," *MotorBoating* (January 1911).

Fergusons: uncles, "Forty-Three Days in an Open Boat," *The Rudder*, May 1910, 392-400, Alexander Crosby Brown, "Isles of Vain Hope," *The Log of Mystic Seaport* (October 1976): 74-85 ; *Christabel* grounding: *New York Times*, June 24, 1909.

Turn of century boating at Fishers: "There isn't a dull moment," *Picturesque Fishers Island: Mansion House and Cottages* (Fishers Island: Fishers Island Farms, n.d.).

Skiddoo, Hay Harbor, and Fishers Island One Design: James F.X. Egan, "Two Harbors: The Story of the Fishers Island One Designs" (1990) and his correspondence with John and Marie Gaillard, provided by Mr. Egan and Mystic Seaport Ships Plans Collection; Marie Gaillard, excerpts from letters to James F.X. Egan and her scrapbook (1980); Howard S. Dodd Jr. to James F.X. Egan, September 26, 1989, Egan collection; FIOD press release, *Brooklyn Eagle*, November 20,

1909; FIOD commissioning, *New York Times*, January 23, 1910, 95; FIOD plans, clippings, and contract in Charles D. Mower Collection, Ships Plans Collection, Mystic Seaport; "He never designed," William H. Taylor, "A Few of Charles D. Mower's Boats," *Yachting* (May 1942); "The Fishers Island Yacht Club have," *The Rudder* (February 1939): 14; "Due to some," Reynolds du Pont to Henry M. Horn, October 6, 1954, FIYC Correspondence General file; dredging, *New York Times*, February 19, 1930, 51.

The second Fishers Island Yacht Club: certificate of incorporation, July 19, 1934, copy in By-Laws file, FIYC Archives; "Simple Facilities," Fishers Island tourist brochure, 1930s, Sara Porter collection.

Schooners and commuters: Robert W. Carrick and Richard Henderson, *John G. Alden and His Yacht Designs* (Camden, Me.: International Marine, 1983); C. Philip Moore, *Yachts in a Hurry: An Illustrated History of the Great Commuter Yachts* (New York: W.W. Norton, n.d.).

Herreshoffs, FIS 31, Herreshoff 23, Bullseye, Luders 16: Maynard Bray and Carlton Pineiro, *Herreshoff of Bristol* (Brooklin, Me.: *WoodenBoat*, 1989); *Yachts by Herreshoff* (Bristol, R.I.: Herreshoff Manufacturing Co., 1935); Alan Bemis, "*Cirrus*: A Treasure from Herreshoff," *WoodenBoat* 34 (May/June 1980): 42-48; David Burnham, articles in *Bullseye Association Newsletter*, February 1998 and March 2003, and in *Fishers Island Gazette*, February 1993; "the Bullseye is just part," Peter Rugg, *Fishers Island Gazette*, February 1989; Robert N. Bavier Jr., "The Luders 16," *Yachting* (April 1948); 1934 American Yacht Club Cruise, *The New York Times*, August 9, 1934; information about L-16, including Luders records, provided by Bob Wallstrom.

Racing in the 1930s: race results and scoring system, 1933-40, Henry L. Ferguson Museum.

Shipwrecks: Robert G. Shanklin, "Wreck of the *Thelma Phoebe*," *The Day*, March 10, 1979; J.P. Morgan wreck, *New York Times*, August 13, 1940.

Chapter III: "There will be Yachting" – 1938-70

1938 Hurricane: Charles B. Ferguson, "Details of Devastation in 1938 Hurricane," *Fishers Island Gazette*, Winter 1997; Everett S. Allen, *A Wind to Shake the World* (Boston: Little, Brown, 1976), 177-78; "The beach used to be white," Cathi Jenssen and Nancy Edwards, "An Interview with Johnny Chestnut (Arasimowicz), *Sea Breezes*, June 1982; Howard S. Dodd Jr. to James F.X. Egan, September 26, 1989, Egan collection; Arthur Whitney letter to FIYC members, November 25, 1938, and Whitney undated report, Sara Porter collection; Maxwell S. Porter correspondence with shipyards, Sara Porter collection; vegetation, Penni Sharp, "Invasive Plant Species Overtaking Native Growth," *Fishers Island Gazette*, Summer 2003; Charles B. Ferguson, "The Cruise of the Little Yawl *Sparrow Hawk*" (1996).

Rhodes 27 and paid hands: *The Rudder* (February 1939): 14; Richard Henderson, *Philip L. Rhodes and His Yacht Designs* (Camden, Me.: International Marine, 1981); R-27 plans in Ships Plans Collection, Mystic Seaport; "I awaited," Bradford Burnham to Yves Gaignet, April 7, 2002; David Burnham to Yves Gaignet, April 3, 2002; David Burnham, "A Boy's Eye View of West Harbor" and "Care Keeps Her Young," *MotorBoating* (May 1956): 44-45, 156-59.

War preparations: Herbert Grandage, "1939 and 1940, Recollections from the Launch Boy" (2002).

Speranza: Hans de Meiss-Teuffen, Log of *Speranza*, 1946, G.W. Blunt White Library, Mystic Seaport; Robert H. Boyle, "Island of the Discreet Shudder," *Sports Illustrated*, September 6, 1965, 40-43,

Commuters: Moore, *Yachts in a Hurry*; Kahn, Jock: *The Life and Times of John Hay Whitney* (New York: Book Sales, 1984), 255-56.

Hurricane Carol: Naval Meteorology and Oceanography Command, "Tropical Cyclones Affecting Groton/New London," http://www.cnmoc.navy.mil/ nmosw/tr8203nc/ nlondon/text/ sect7.htm.

Off Soundings Club and Parsons Trophy: *History of the Off Soundings Club* (1984), and http://www.offsoundings.org.; *Westerly Sun*, August 5, 2002, http://www.whyc.net/ 2002parsonscup.html.

Brown family, *Bolero*: "comfortable cruising yacht," "Admired as," Olin J. Stephens II, *Lines: A Half-Century of Yacht Designs by Sparkman & Stephens, 1930-1980* (Jaffrey, N.H.: Godine, 2003).

Pete du Pont: Bill Robinson, *A Berth to Bermuda* (Princeton: D. Van Nostrand, 1961); names of skippers, Owen C. Smith.

Captain Johan Johansen: "Cap. John Celebrates His 100th Birthday in Florida," *Fishers Island Gazette*, August 1991.

Ed Hedge: Bertha S. Hedge to M.S. Porter, May 1, 1966; Porter to Hedge, May 5, 1966; bill, Hedge to Porter, June 13, 1966, all in Sara Porter collection.

Launch boys: Grandage, "1939 and 1940, Recollections from the Launch Boy."

Chapter IV: "The Energy within the Club" – 1970-95

1970s: Eliot Porter farewell speech, minutes of 1973 annual meeting, FIYC 1973 Correspondence file, FIYC Archives; 'Round Island Race, minutes annual meeting, 1974 Correspondence file, FIYC Archives; uniforms, Burton G. Tremaine Jr., to Richard E. Riegel Jr., April 18, 1974, 1974 Correspondence file, FIYC Archives; Kinsolving opening day prayer, posted in FIYC.

Bullseyes: Daniel Spurr, *Heart of Glass: Fiberglass Boats and the Men Who Made Them* (Camden, Me.: International Marine/McGraw-Hill, 2000); George Warren Smith to Burton G. Tremaine Jr., December 1, 1969, Eliot Porter to Smith, March 30, 1970, Smith to Porter, April 1, 1970, Sara Porter collection; National Championship results, http:// www2. primushost.com / ~bullseye.

Storms: Daniela Altimari, "The Blizzard of '78," *Hartford Courant*, February 25, 1998; "Cap. John Celebrates His 100th Birthday in Florida," *Fishers Island Gazette*, August 1991; "Eyewitnesses," *International One Design World Class News*, Spring 1992.

1988 wrecks: "Rocky Reception for Two Boats," Fishers Island Gazette, October 1988.

Junior program: Rugg proposal, "Plan to Expand Junior Sailing Program," August 1985, FIYC Archives.

Fishing: Bob Miller's "On the Hook" columns in *Fishers Island Gazette*: "Ospreys," May 1988, "sizeable bass" and "on May 6," October 1988; Charles B. Ferguson, "The Classic," *Fishers Island Gazette*, Spring 1994.

International One Design: Boots Wright, Peter Rugg, "Islander Finishes Third in Transatlantic Race," *Fishers Island Gazette*, August 1990; John Burnham, "A Champion's View from the Tiller," *Fishers Island Gazette*, Fall 1996.

History Committee Acknowledgments

For most of his tenure as commodore, John Brim pressed the board of governors to invest in a history of the club. What were the stories behind the photos of the boats and models on the clubhouse walls? How long had sailors been dodging the Clumps and tacking against the current on Fishers Island Sound?

In 2001, with a history committee assembled and Walter Keenan as commodore, the board took the leap and hired John Rousmaniere as author. Even though the club turned out to be much younger than we had thought and its records were far from complete, John's next two summers proved eventful as he began uncovering the story, assisted on his several visits to the island by committee members Dave Burnham, Sara Porter, Harris Parsons, Charlie Ferguson, and Commodore Keenan.

John wrote the book as dozens of short stories about sailors and boats, intending to illustrate it with plenty of photos. When Mystic Seaport signed on as our co-publisher, we gained momentum, thanks to Mary Ann Stets and Andy German, who, respectively, plumbed the Museum's Rosenfeld photo collection and took over primary editorial navigation. Finally, Darcy Magratten, our designer, made this book what we all hoped it would be—both extremely attractive and highly readable.

A sincere thank you to all who played a role in this book's creation, especially my fellow committee members and, in the final push, Commodore Bill Reed, Lisa Reed, and Elisabeth Bohlen. But above all, thanks to John Rousmaniere, who sold us on writing a book about Sailing at Fishers instead of a narrow club history. That decision was spot on and would have made perfect sense to the club's founding members. Like us, they were motivated less by a desire to build an institution of great stature than by a simple wish to spend time together, sailing at Fishers Island.

John S. Burnham

Fishers Island Yacht Club History Committee

INDEX

Page numbers of illustrations appear in bold type

R

S

T

U

V

W

Y

Z

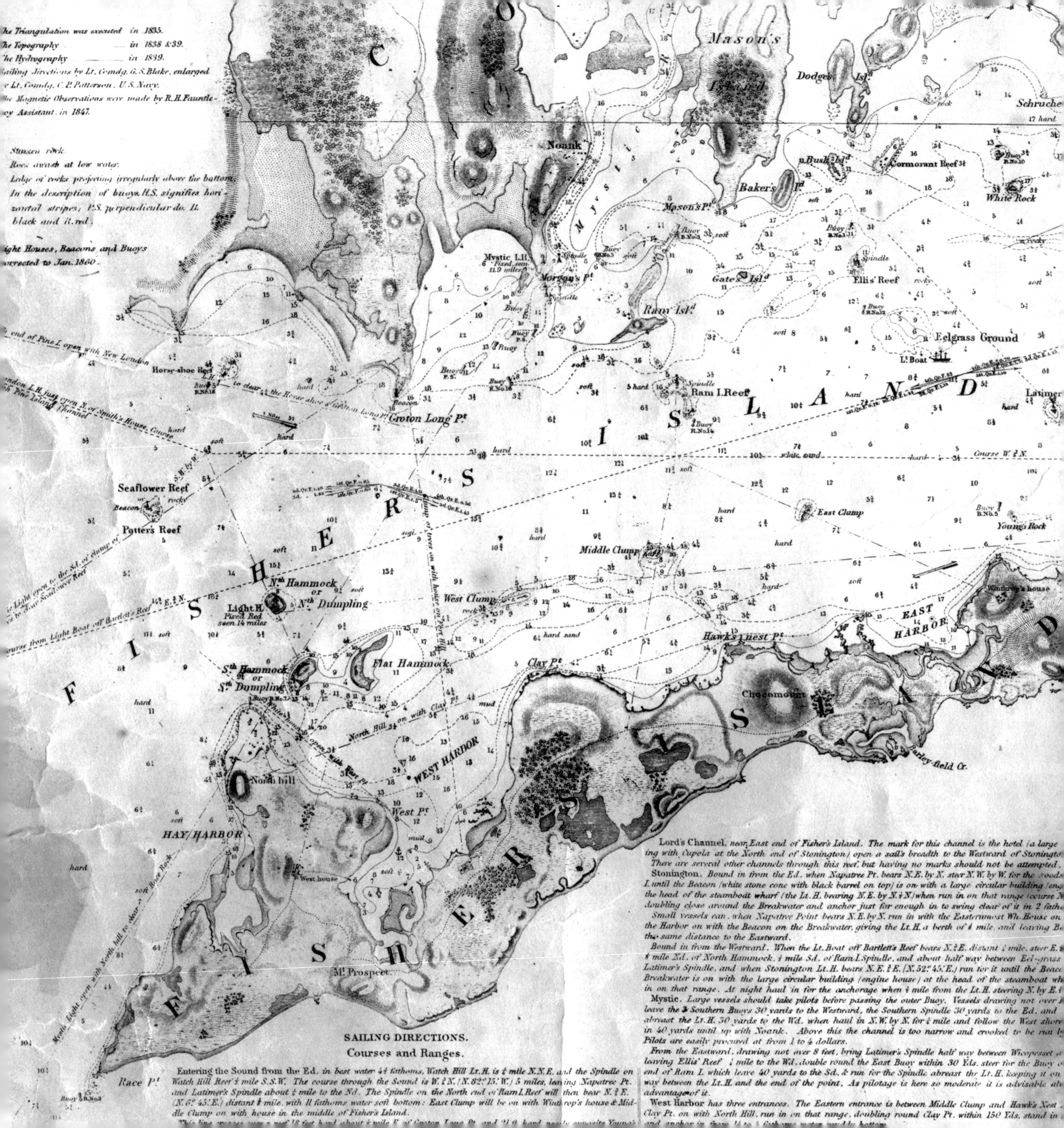

SAILING DIRECTIONS.

Courses and Ranges.

Entering the Sound from the Ed. *in best water 4½ fathoms, Watch Hill Lt. H. is ¼ mile N.N.E. and the Spindle on Watch Hill Reef ½ mile S.S.W. The course through the Sound is W. ¾ N. (N. 82° 15′ W.) 5 miles, leaving Napatree Pt. and Latimer's Spindle about ¼ mile to the Nd. The Spindle on the North end of Ram I. Reef will then bear N. ¾ E. (N. 6° 45′ E.) distant ¼ mile, with 11 fathoms water soft bottom: East Clump will be on with Winthrop's house & Middle Clump on with house in the middle of Fisher's Island.*

Lord's Channel, *near East end of Fisher's Island. The mark for this channel is the hotel (a large ... ing with Cupola at the North end of Stonington) open a sail's breadth to the Westward of Stonington ... There are several other channels through this reef, but having no marks should not be attempted.*

Stonington. *Bound in from the Ed. when Napatree Pt. bears N.E. by N. steer N.W. by W. for the Woods I. until the Beacon (white stone cone with black barrel on top) is on with a large circular building (eng... the head of the steamboat wharf (the Lt. H. bearing N.E. by N. ¼ N.) when run in on that range (course N... doubling close around the Breakwater and anchor just far enough in to swing clear of it in 2 fath...*

Small vessels can, when Napatree Point bears N.E. by N. run in with the Easternmost Wh. House on the Harbor on with the Beacon on the Breakwater, giving the Lt. H. a berth of ¼ mile, and leaving B... the same distance to the Eastward.

Bound in from the Westward. When the Lt. Boat off Bartlett's Reef bears N. ¾ E. distant ¼ mile, steer E. ... ¼ mile Nd. of North Hammock, ¼ mile Sd. of Ram I. Spindle, and about half way between Eel-grass ... Latimer's Spindle, and when Stonington Lt. H. bears N.E. ¾ E. (N. 52° 45′ E.) run for it until the Beac... Breakwater is on with the large circular building (engine house) at the head of the steamboat wh... in on that range. At night haul in for the anchorage when ¼ mile from the Lt. H. steering N. by E. ...

Mystic. *Large vessels should take pilots before passing the outer Buoy. Vessels drawing not over ... leave the 3 Southern Buoys 30 yards to the Westward, the Southern Spindle 30 yards to the Ed. and ... abreast the Lt. H. 30 yards to the Wd. when haul in N.W. by N. for ¼ mile and follow the West shore ... in 40 yards until up with Noank. Above this the channel is too narrow and crooked to be run b... Pilots are easily procured at from 1 to 4 dollars.*

From the Eastward, drawing not over 8 feet, bring Latimer's Spindle half way between Wicopesset a... leaving Ellis' Reef ¼ mile to the Wd. double round the East Buoy within 30 Yds. steer for the Buoy ... end of Ram I. which leave 40 yards to the Sd. & run for the Spindle abreast the Lt. H. keeping it on ... way between the Lt. H. and the end of the point. As pilotage is here so moderate it is advisable al... advantage of it.

West Harbor *has three entrances. The Eastern entrance is between Middle Clump and Hawk's Nest ... Clay Pt. on with North Hill, run in on that range, doubling round Clay Pt. within 150 Yds. stand in ...*